i

TRADE BARRIERS AND CHINA

MARTHA B. KESSLER

Nova Science Publishers, Inc.
New York

For permission to use material from this book please contact us:
Telephone 631-231-7269; Fax 631-231-8175
Web Site: http://www.novapublishers.com

LIBRARY OF CONGRESS CATALOGING-IN-PUBLICATION DATA

Kessler, Martha B.
Trade barriers and China / Martha B. Kessler.
p. cm.
ISBN 978-1-60456-686-4 (softcover)
1. China--Commercial policy. 2. Foreign trade regulation--China. 3. Non-tariff trade barriers--China. 4. Protectionism--China. 5. China--Foreign economic relations. I. Title.
HF1604.K47 2008
382'.50951--dc22

2008015180

Published by Nova Science Publishers, Inc.; New York

CONTENTS

PREFACE

China has taken significant and often impressive steps to reform its economy since acceding to the WTO. During this period, China has repealed, revised or enacted more than one thousand laws, regulations and other measures in an effort to bring its trading system into basic compliance with WTO standards. China has also taken steps to implement numerous specific commitments pursuant to schedules set forth in its WTO accession agreement. Each year, China has made annual reductions in its tariff rates, eliminated non-tariff barriers, expanded market access for foreign services providers and improved transparency. All of these steps were designed to deepen China's integration into the international trading system, as well as to facilitate and strengthen economic reforms that China had begun 20 years earlier.

Chapter 1

TRADE SUMMARY

The U.S. goods trade deficit with China was $232.5 billion in 2006, an increase of $31 billion from $201.5 billion in 2005. U.S. goods exports in 2006 were $55.2 billion, up 31.7 percent from the previous year. Corresponding U.S. imports from China were $287.8 billion, up 18.2 percent. China is currently the 4th largest export market for U.S. goods.

U.S. exports of private commercial services (i.e., excluding military and government) to China were $9.1 billion in 2005 (latest data available), and U.S. imports were $6.5 billion. Sales of services in China by majority U.S.-owned affiliates were $5.1 billion in 2004 (latest data available), while sales of services in the United States by majority China-owned firms were not available in 2004 ($321 million in 2002 is latest data available).

The stock of U.S. foreign direct investment (FDI) in China in 2005 was $16.9 billion (latest data available), up from $15.0 billion in 2004. U.S. FDI in China is concentrated largely in the manufacturing, wholesale trade, mining and non-bank holding companies sectors.

When China acceded to the World Trade Organization (WTO) on December 11, 2001, it committed to implement over time a set of sweeping reforms that required it to lower trade barriers in virtually every sector of the economy, provide national treatment and improved market access to goods and services imported from the United States and other WTO Members, and protect intellectual property rights (IPR). Five years later, the deadlines for almost all of China's commitments have passed, and China's transition period as a new WTO Member is now essentially over.

China has taken significant and often impressive steps to reform its economy since acceding to the WTO. During this period, China has repealed, revised or enacted more than one thousand laws, regulations and other measures in an effort to bring its trading system into basic compliance with WTO standards. China has also taken steps to implement numerous specific commitments pursuant to schedules set forth in its WTO accession agreement. Each year, China has made annual reductions in its tariff rates, eliminated non-tariff barriers, expanded market access for foreign services providers and improved transparency. All of these steps were designed to deepen China's integration into the international trading system, as well as to facilitate and strengthen economic reforms that China had begun 20 years earlier.

Nevertheless, despite significant progress in many areas, China's record in implementing WTO commitments is decidedly mixed. China continues to pursue problematic industrial policies that rely on trade-distorting measures such as local content requirements, import and export restrictions, discriminatory regulations and prohibited subsidies, all of which raise serious WTO concerns. China's shortcomings in enforcing laws in areas where detailed WTO disciplines apply, such as intellectual property rights, have also created serious problems for the United States and its other trading partners.

Many of the United States' most difficult trade issues with China can be traced to excessive Chinese government intervention in the market through policy directives and the actions of individual officials. This government intervention, evident in many areas of China's economy, is a reflection of China's historic yet unfinished transition from a centrally planned economy to a free-market economy governed by rule of law. To some extent, these difficulties were anticipated. During the fifteen years of negotiations leading up to China's WTO accession, the United States and other WTO Members were aware of the state's large role in China's economy and carefully negotiated conditions for China's WTO accession that would, when implemented, lead to significantly reduced levels of government intervention in the market, and a corresponding reduction in trade distortions and market access barriers.

While China did make noteworthy progress as a result of economic reforms adopted before and in the first few years after its accession to the WTO, recently we have seen an upsurge in industrial planning measures as tools of economic development by China's central government authorities. China appears to want to expand the government's role in directing the economy and in developing internationally competitive Chinese enterprises, while also restricting the role of international companies in certain sectors.

Recognizing these challenges, USTR announced, in a "top-to-bottom" review of U.S.-China trade relations issued in February 2006, that it would adopt a dual-track approach to resolving its WTO concerns. The United States would continue to seek cooperative and pragmatic resolutions through bilateral dialogue with China, including the Joint Commission on Commerce and Trade (JCCT), as well as *ad hoc* bilateral meetings and a variety of sector-specific dialogues. However, when bilateral dialogue fails to succeed in addressing U.S. concerns, the United States will not hesitate to exercise its WTO rights through the initiation of dispute settlement against China, as it would with any other mature WTO trading partner.

The United States achieved some important successes through bilateral dialogue in 2006, including at a JCCT meeting in April. At that meeting, China made several commitments related to IPR protection and enforcement. It also committed to eliminate duplicative testing and certification requirements applicable to imported medical devices, to make adjustments to its registered capital requirements for telecommunications service providers and to finalize a protocol allowing the resumption of trade in U.S. beef and beef products. China also reaffirmed past commitments to technology neutrality for 3G telecommunications standards and to ensuring that foreign express couriers would not be impacted negatively by new rules in the postal area. In addition, China committed to commence, by no later than December 31, 2007, formal negotiations to join the WTO's Government Procurement Agreement. Since the JCCT meeting in April 2006, the United States has been working with China to make sure that it implements all of these commitments.

However, to date, other issues have evaded bilateral resolution, despite extensive dialogue. Issues like WTO-prohibited subsidies, IPR enforcement and certain market access concerns have resisted resolution. Although the United States has been making earnest efforts to resolve these concerns through bilateral discussions, it is prepared to pursue other options if the bilateral approach is not fruitful, as it recently did when it initiated a WTO dispute settlement case challenging apparent WTO-prohibited subsidies.

In several areas, Chinese policies and practices continued to cause particular concern for the United States and U.S. industry in 2006, particularly in light of China's WTO commitments, as is detailed below and in the 2006 USTR Report to Congress on China's WTO Compliance. First, the lack of effective IPR enforcement remains a major challenge, as counterfeiting and piracy in China remain at unacceptably high levels and cause serious economic harm to U.S. businesses in virtually every sector of the economy. Second, China has continued to resort to industrial policies that limit market access for non-Chinese origin goods and foreign service providers, and that provide substantial government resources to support Chinese industries and increase exports. Third, capricious practices by Chinese customs and quarantine officials can delay or halt shipments of agricultural products into China, while sanitary and phytosanitary standards with questionable scientific bases and a generally opaque regulatory regime frequently bedevil traders in agricultural commodities. Fourth, Chinese regulatory authorities continue to frustrate efforts of

U.S. providers of banking, insurance, motor vehicle financing, direct selling, telecommunications, construction and engineering, legal and other services to achieve their full market potential in China through the use of an opaque regulatory process, overly burdensome licensing and operating requirements, and other means. They have also imposed new restrictions on foreign providers of financial information services and have so far failed to open up the China market to foreign credit card companies. Fifth, transparency remains a concern, as many of China's regulatory regimes continued to suffer from systemic opacity, frustrating efforts of foreign – and domestic – businesses to achieve the potential benefits of China's WTO accession.

Overall, while China has a more open and competitive economy than 25 years ago, and China's WTO accession has led to the removal of many trade barriers, there are still barriers to trade that have yet to be dismantled. The central government continues to implement industrial policies that protect a number of noncompetitive or emerging sectors of the economy from foreign competition. In many sectors, import barriers, opaque and inconsistently applied legal provisions and limitations on foreign direct investment often combine to make it difficult for foreign firms to operate in China. In addition, some ministries, agencies and government-sponsored trade associations have renewed efforts to erect new technical barriers to trade. Meanwhile, many provincial governments at times have strongly resisted reforms that would eliminate sheltered markets for local enterprises or reduce jobs and revenues in their jurisdictions, although they have also supported market access for other foreign investors that do not pose a threat to local vested interests.

To meet its obligations as a responsible stakeholder in the world trading system, China will need to institutionalize market-oriented reforms and eliminate mechanisms that allow government officials to intervene in the Chinese economy in a manner that is inconsistent with market principles. China also needs to take additional steps to make its trade regime more predictable and transparent. Despite its remarkable transformation over the past quarter century, China continues to suffer from its command economy legacy, and Chinese government policymaking often operates in a way that prevents U.S. businesses from achieving their full potential in the China market. Through the new high-level Strategic Economic Dialogue launched in December 2006 and ongoing bilateral dialogues like the JCCT, the United States is pushing China to accelerate its transformation into a more market-based economy.

Chapter 2

IMPORT BARRIERS

Prior to its WTO accession in December 2001, China restricted imports through high tariffs and taxes, quotas and other non-tariff measures, and restrictions on trading rights. Beginning in 2002, its first year in the WTO, China significantly reduced tariff rates on many products, decreased the number of goods subject to import quotas, expanded trading rights for Chinese enterprises and increased the transparency of its licensing procedures. Subsequently, China has continued to make progress by implementing tariff reductions on schedule, phasing out import quotas and expanding trading rights for foreign enterprises and individuals. Nevertheless, some serious problems remain, such as China's tariff treatment of imported automotive parts and China's refusal to grant trading rights for certain industries.

Trading Rights

Prior to its WTO accession, China restricted the types and numbers of entities with the right to trade. Only those domestic and foreign firms with trading rights could import goods into, or export goods out of, China. Restrictions on the type and number of firms with trading rights contributed to systemic inefficiencies in China's trading rights system and created substantial incentives to engage in smuggling and other corrupt practices.

In 1995, liberalization of China's trading rights system began to proceed gradually. The pace accelerated in 1999 when the Ministry of Foreign Trade and Economic Cooperation (MOFTEC), the predecessor to China's existing Ministry of Commerce (MOFCOM), announced new guidelines allowing a wide variety of

Chinese firms with annual export volumes valued in excess of $10 million to register for trading rights. In August 2001, China extended this regulation to allow foreign-invested firms to export their finished products. Import rights for foreign-invested firms were still restricted to the importation of inputs, equipment and other materials directly related to their manufacturing or processing operations. Firms and individuals without trading rights, including foreign-invested firms with a manufacturing presence in China seeking to import products made outside of China, were required to use a local agent.

In its WTO accession agreement, China committed to substantial liberalization in the area of trading rights. Specifically, China committed to eliminate its system of examination and approval of trading rights and to make full trading rights automatically available to all Chinese enterprises, Chinese-foreign joint ventures, wholly foreign-owned enterprises and foreign individuals, including sole proprietorships, within three years of its accession, or by December 11, 2004, which was the same deadline for China to eliminate most restrictions in the area of distribution services. China further committed to expand the availability of trading rights pursuant to an agreed schedule during the first three years of its WTO membership.

Although China did not fully adhere to the agreed phase-in schedule in some instances, it put in place a registration system implementing the required liberalization of trading rights, both for Chinese enterprises and for Chinese-foreign joint ventures, wholly foreign-owned enterprises and foreign individuals, including sole proprietorships. This liberalization is reflected in China's revised Foreign Trade Law, issued in April 2004. It provides for trading rights to be automatically available through a registration process for all domestic and foreign entities and individuals, effective July 1, 2004, almost six months ahead of the scheduled full liberalization required by China's accession agreement. In June 2004, MOFCOM issued implementing rules establishing the procedures for registering as a foreign trade operator. U.S. companies have reported few problems with the new trading rights registration process.

In December 2004, as required by its WTO accession agreement, China also ended its practice of granting import rights or export rights for certain products, including steel, natural rubber, wools, acrylic and plywood, only to designated enterprises. Any domestic or foreign enterprise or individual can now trade in these products.

Consistent with the terms of China's WTO accession agreement, the importation of some goods, such as petroleum and sugar, is still reserved for state-trading enterprises. In addition, for goods still subject to tariff-rate quotas such as grains, cotton, vegetable oils and fertilizers, China reserves a portion of the in-quota imports for state-trading enterprises, while it committed to make the remaining portion (ranging from 10 percent to 90 percent, depending on the commodity) available for importation through non-state traders. In some cases, the percentage available to non-state traders increases annually for a fixed number of years.

Meanwhile, however, China has not yet given foreign entities trading rights for the importation of books, newspapers, periodicals, electronic publications and audio and video products. Under the terms of China's accession agreement, China's trading rights commitments appear to apply fully to these products, as they are not among the products for which China reserved the right to engage in state trading. As a result, trading rights for these products should have been automatically available to all Chinese enterprises, Chinese-foreign joint ventures, wholly foreign-owned enterprises and foreign individuals as of December 11, 2004. Nevertheless, China continues to wholly reserve the right to import books, newspapers, periodicals, electronic publications and audio and video products to state trading enterprises.

Import Substitution Policies

Throughout the 1990s, China gradually reduced formal import substitution policies. When it acceded to the WTO, China agreed to eliminate all subsidies prohibited under Article 3 of the WTO Agreement on Subsidies and Countervailing Measures (Subsidies Agreement), including all forms of subsidies contingent on the use of domestic over imported goods. In its WTO accession agreement, China also committed that it would not condition import or investment approvals on whether there are competing domestic suppliers or impose other performance requirements. In anticipation of this commitment, China enacted legal changes in 2000 and 2001 to eliminate local content requirements for foreign investments. Under the prevailing rules, however, investors are still "encouraged" to follow some of the formerly mandated practices. Instances in which the Chinese government has reportedly pursued import substitution or similar policies are described below.

Corporate Tax Deductions to Foreign-Invested Firms

Measures issued by the Ministry of Finance and the State Administration for Taxation (SAT) make income tax and value-added tax (VAT) refunds available to foreign-invested firms in connection with their purchases of domestically manufactured equipment. These refunds are not available in connection with purchases of imported equipment or equipment assembled in China from imported parts. A similar measure makes an income tax refund available in connection with domestic firms' purchases of domestically manufactured equipment for technology upgrading.

Automotive Parts

Before China's WTO accession, China's automobile industrial policy offered significant advantages for foreign-invested factories using high levels of local content. In 2001, in anticipation of China's new obligations as a WTO Member, the State Economic and Trade Commission (SETC) issued Bulletin No.13, which provided that the preferential policy for automobile localization rates would be cancelled upon China's WTO accession. However, U.S. automobile manufacturers reported that some local government officials continued to require local content and cited the old automobile industrial policy's standards. China also committed to issue a revised automotive industrial policy within two years of its WTO accession, or by December 11, 2003, but missed this deadline. In May 2004, China issued a new automobile industrial policy. It included provisions discouraging the importation of automotive parts and encouraging the use of domestic technology. It also required new automobile and automobile engine plants to include substantial investment in research and development facilities, even though China expressly committed in its WTO accession agreement not to condition investment rights or approvals on the conduct of research and development in China.

In 2005, China began to issue measures implementing the new automobile industrial policy. One measure that generated strong criticism from the United States, the EU, Japan and Canada was the *Measures on the Importation of Parts for Entire Automobiles*, which was issued by the National Development and Reform Commission (NDRC) in February 2005 and became effective in April 2005. These rules impose charges that unfairly discriminate against imported automotive parts and discourage automobile manufacturers in China from using imported automotive parts in the assembly of vehicles. Specifically, the rules require all vehicle manufacturers in China that use imported parts to register with China's Customs Administration and provide specific information about each vehicle they assemble, including a list of the imported and domestic parts to be used, and the value and supplier of each part. If the number or value of imported parts in an assembled vehicle exceeds specified thresholds, the regulations assess each of the imported parts a charge equal to the tariff on complete automobiles (typically 25 percent) rather than the tariff applicable to automotive parts (typically 10 percent). These rules appear to be inconsistent with several WTO provisions, including Article III of GATT 1994 and Article 2 of the Agreement on Trade-Related Investment Measures, as well as the commitment in China's accession agreement to eliminate all local content requirements relating to importation. In March and April 2006, the United States, the EU and Canada initiated dispute settlement against China by filing formal WTO consultations requests. Joint consultations were held in May 2006. However, these consultations did not lead to an agreed resolution. In September 2006, the United States, the EU and Canada filed requests for the establishment of a panel to hear the dispute. A panel was established at the October 2006 meeting of the WTO's Dispute Settlement Body.

Steel

China issued a new Steel and Iron Industry Development Policy in July 2005. Although many aspects of this new policy have not yet been implemented, it still includes a host of objectives and guidelines that raise serious concerns. For example, this policy requires that foreign enterprises seeking to invest in Chinese iron and steel enterprises possess proprietary technology or intellectual property in the processing of steel. Given that foreign investors are not allowed to have a controlling share in steel and iron enterprises in China, this requirement would seem to constitute a *de facto* technology transfer requirement, calling into question China's implementation of its WTO accession agreement commitment not to condition investment rights or approvals on the transfer of technology. This policy also appears to discriminate against foreign equipment and technology imports. Like other measures, this policy encourages the use of local content by calling for a variety of government financial support for steel and iron projects utilizing newly developed domestic equipment. Even more troubling, however, it calls for the use of domestically-produced steel-manufacturing equipment and domestic technologies whenever domestic suppliers exist, calling into question China's implementation of its WTO accession agreement commitment not to condition the right of investment or importation on whether competing domestic suppliers exist.

Semiconductors

China's 10th Five-Year Plan calls for an increase in Chinese semiconductor output from $2 billion in 2000 to $24 billion in 2010. In pursuit of this policy, China has attempted to encourage the development of China's domestic integrated circuit (IC) industry through, among other things, discriminatory VAT policies. In particular, through a series of measures, China has provided for the rebate of a substantial portion of the 17 percent VAT paid by domestic manufacturers on their locally-produced ICs. China, meanwhile, charged the full 17 percent VAT on imported ICs, unless they were designed in China. After bilateral meetings on this issue failed to yield a change in China's policy, in March 2004, the United States filed the first WTO case against China. In the ensuing consultations, China signaled its willingness to discuss a possible resolution. In July 2004, the United States and China reached a settlement in which China agreed to immediately cease certifying new Chinese IC manufacturers or products as eligible for the VAT rebate and to issue the necessary regulations to eliminate the VAT rebate entirely by November 1, 2004, with an effective date no later than April 1, 2005. China also agreed to repeal the relevant implementing rules that had made VAT rebates available for ICs designed in China but manufactured abroad by September 1, 2004, with an effective date no later than October 1, 2004. China followed through on each of these agreed steps in a timely manner, and the two sides notified the WTO in October 2005 that their dispute had been satisfactorily resolved. Nevertheless, the United States continues to monitor closely new financial support that China is making available to its domestic producers for consistency with the WTO Subsidies Agreement's disciplines.

Fertilizer

In 2001, China began exempting all phosphate fertilizers except diammonium phosphate (DAP) from the VAT. DAP, a product that the United States exports to China, competes with other phosphate fertilizers produced in China, particularly monoammonium phosphate. Both the United States Government and U.S. producers have complained that China has employed its VAT policies to benefit domestic fertilizer production.

Telecommunications Equipment

There have been continuing reports of the Ministry of Information Industry (MII) and China Telecom adopting policies to discourage the use of imported components or equipment. For example, MII has reportedly still not rescinded an internal circular issued in 1998 instructing telecommunications companies to buy components and equipment from domestic sources.

Tariffs and other Import Charges

Under the terms of its WTO accession, China committed to substantial annual reductions in its tariff rates, with most of them taking place within five years of China's WTO accession. The largest reductions took place in 2002, immediately after China acceded to the WTO, when the overall average tariff rate fell from over 15 percent to 12 percent.

China's post-WTO accession tariff rates are "bound," meaning that China cannot raise them above the bound rates without "compensating" WTO trading partners (i.e.: re-balancing tariff concessions or, in accordance with WTO rules, being subject to withdrawal of substantially equivalent concessions by other WTO Members). "Bound" rates give importers a more predictable environment. China may also apply tariff rates significantly lower than the WTO-required rate, as in the case of goods that the government has identified as necessary to the development of a key industry. For example, China's Customs Administration has occasionally announced lower applied tariff rates for items that benefit key economic sectors, in particular for the automotive, steel and chemical industries.

U.S. exports continued to benefit from China's participation in the Information Technology Agreement (ITA), which requires the elimination of tariffs on computers, semiconductors and other information technology products. China began reducing and eliminating these tariffs in 2002 and continued to do so in the ensuing years, achieving the elimination of all ITA tariffs on January 1, 2005, as the tariffs dropped to zero from a pre-WTO accession average of 13.3 percent. U.S. exports of ITA goods continued to perform well in 2006, as they totaled $9.2 billion, an increase of 52 percent over the 2005 figure.

China completed its timely implementation of another significant tariff initiative, the WTO's Chemical Tariff Harmonization Agreement, in 2005. The United States exported $6.5 billion in chemicals to China in 2006, up from $5.6 billion in 2005, an increase of 16.7 percent.

However, China still maintains high duties on some products that compete with sensitive domestic industries. For example, the tariff on large motorcycles will only fall from 60 percent to 45 percent. Likewise, most video, digital video and audio recorders and players still face duties of approximately 30 percent. Raisins face duties of 35 percent.

U.S. exports of some bulk agricultural commodities have increased dramatically in recent years, and continue to perform strongly, especially soybeans and cotton. Exports of soybeans rose to more than $2.5 billion in 2006, a 12 percent increase over the previous year. Cotton exports rose 47 percent in the same period to nearly $2.1 billion, a new record. Exports of forest products such as lumber also continued to perform strongly, increasing by 16 percent over 2005, to reach $547 million in 2006. Fish and seafood exports rose 25 percent to $440 million in 2006. Meanwhile, exports of consumer-oriented agricultural products increased by 34 percent to $731 million in 2006.

Overall, China's tariff changes have increased market access for U.S. exporters in a range of industries, as China continued the process of reducing tariffs on goods of greatest importance to U.S. industry from a base average of 25 percent (in 1997) to 7 percent over a period of five years, starting on January 1, 2002. It made similar reductions throughout the agricultural sector. These tariff changes contributed to another significant increase in overall U.S. exports, which rose approximately 33 percent from January through December 2006, when compared to the same time period in 2005.

Tariff Classification

Chinese customs officers have wide discretion in classifying a particular import. While foreign businesses might at times have benefited from their ability to negotiate tariff classification into tariff categories with lower import duty rates, lack of uniformity makes it difficult to anticipate border charges.

Customs Valuation

In January 2002, shortly after acceding to the WTO, China's Customs Administration issued the Measures for Examining and Determining Customs Valuation of Imported Goods. These regulations addressed the inconsistencies that had existed between China's customs valuation methodologies and the WTO Agreement on Customs Valuation. The Customs Administration subsequently issued the Rules on the Determination of Customs Value of Royalties and License Fees Related to Imported Goods, effective July 2003. These rules were intended to clarify provisions of the January 2002 regulations that addressed the valuation of royalties and license fees. In addition, by December 11, 2003, China had issued a measure on interest charges and a measure requiring duties on software to be assessed on the basis of the value of the underlying carrier medium, meaning, for example, the CD-ROM or floppy disk itself, rather than the imputed value of the content, which includes, for example, the data recorded on a CD-ROM or floppy disk.

More than three years later, China has still not uniformly implemented these various measures. U.S. exporters continue to report that they are encountering valuation problems at many ports. According to U.S. exporters, although the 2002 regulations and 2003 implementing rules provide that imported goods normally should be valued on the basis of their transaction price, meaning the price the importer actually paid, many Chinese customs officials are still improperly using "reference pricing," which usually results in a higher dutiable value. For example, imports of wood products are often subjected to reference pricing. In addition, some of China's customs officials are reportedly not applying the provisions in the 2002 regulations and 2003 implementing rules as they relate to software royalties and license fees. Following their pre-WTO accession practice, these officials are still automatically adding royalties and license fees to the dutiable value (for example, when an imported personal computer includes pre-installed software), even though China's 2003 implementing rules expressly direct them to add those fees only if they are import-related and a condition of sale for the goods being valued.

U.S. exporters have also continued to express concerns about the Customs Administration's handling of imports of digital media that contain instructions for the subsequent production of multiple copies of products such as DVDs. The Customs Administration has been inappropriately assessing duties based on the estimated value of the yet-to-be-produced copies.

More generally, U.S. exporters continue to be concerned about inefficient and inconsistent customs clearance procedures in China. These procedures vary from port to port, massive delays are not uncommon, and the fees charged appear to be excessive and are rising rapidly, giving rise to concerns about China's compliance with its obligations under Article VIII of GATT 1994.

Rules of Origin

In September 2004, nearly three years after China acceded to the WTO, the State Council finally issued the regulations intended to bring China's rules of origin into conformity with WTO rules for import and export purposes. These regulations took effect on January 1, 2005. Importers have not reported problems stemming from inappropriate application of rules of origin.

Border Trade

China's border trade policy continues to generate MFN and other concerns. China provides preferential import duty and VAT treatment to certain products, often from Russia, apparently even when those products are not confined to frontier traffic as envisioned by Article XXIV of GATT 1994. China addressed some of these concerns in 2003 when it eliminated preferential treatment for boric acid and 19 other products. Nonetheless, it appears that large operators are still able to take advantage of border trade policies to import bulk shipments across China's land borders into its interior at preferential rates. In addition, U.S. industry reports that China continues to use border trade policies to provide preferential treatment for Russian timber imports, to the detriment of U.S. timber exporters.

Antidumping, Countervailing Duty and Safeguard Measures

Since acceding to the WTO, China has emerged as a significant user of antidumping measures, with a total of 91 antidumping measures in place affecting imports from 21 countries, and 17 antidumping investigations in progress, by the end of 2006. China continued to actively apply its antidumping law in 2006, initiating several new investigations, although none of them involved U.S. products. Chemical products remain the most frequent target of Chinese antidumping actions.

Most of the rules and regulations used by MOFCOM to conduct its antidumping investigations were issued as provisional measures by MOFCOM's predecessor agencies – MOFTEC and SETC – shortly after China acceded to the WTO. While these measures generally represent good-faith efforts to implement the relevant WTO commitments and to improve China's pre-WTO accession measures, they also contain vague language, have gaps in areas of practice and allow inordinate discretion. Meanwhile, China's handling of antidumping investigations and reviews continues to raise concerns in key areas such as transparency and procedural fairness. Concerns with transparency, including access to information, are especially acute with regard to the injury portion of investigations.

To date, China has not initiated a countervailing duty investigation. China's only safeguard measure was removed at the end of 2003 after being in place for less than two years.

The Supreme People's Court has issued a judicial interpretation covering the review of antidumping and other trade remedy decisions. To date, however, judicial review of these types of decisions remains untested.

In one antidumping investigation involving imports of kraft linerboard from the United States, following an affirmative final determination and the imposition of antidumping duties in September 2005, the affected U.S. exporters filed for administrative reconsideration with MOFCOM. The exporters raised concerns with various aspects of the final determination, particularly the injury finding. In

January 2006, immediately after the United States notified China that it intended to commence dispute settlement at the WTO, MOFCOM issued a decision repealing the antidumping order.

Non-Tariff Barriers

China's WTO accession agreement obligated China to address many of the non-tariff barriers it had historically used to restrict trade. For example, China is obligated to phase out its import quota system, apply international norms to its testing and standards administration, remove local content requirements, and make its licensing and registration regimes transparent. At the national level, China made progress following its WTO accession in reforming its testing system, revising regulations requiring local content and improving overall regulatory transparency, including in the licensing area. Despite this progress, however, as China's trade liberalization efforts moved forward, some non-tariff barriers remained in place and others were added.

Five years after China's WTO accession, many U.S. industries complain that they face significant non-tariff barriers to trade, which are discussed in more detail in various sections below. These barriers include, for example, regulations that set high thresholds for entry into service sectors such as banking, insurance and telecommunications, selective and unwarranted inspection requirements for agricultural imports and the use of questionable sanitary and phytosanitary measures to control import volumes. Many U.S. industries have also complained about China's manipulation of technical regulations and standards to favor domestic industries.

Import Quotas

In the past, China often did not announce import quota amounts or the process for allocating import quotas. China set import quotas through negotiations between central and local government officials at the end of each year. Import quotas on most products were eliminated or are scheduled for phase-out under the terms of China's WTO accession. China's accession agreement required China to eliminate existing import quotas for the top U.S. priority products upon accession and to phase out remaining import quotas on industrial goods, such as air conditioners, sound and video recording machines, color TVs, cameras, watches, crane lorries and chassis, and motorcycles, by January 1, 2005. While China's post-WTO accession import quota system was beset with problems, China did fully adhere to the agreed schedule for the elimination of all of its import quotas, the last of which China eliminated on January 1, 2005.

Tariff-Rate Quotas

In 1996, China claimed to have introduced a tariff-rate quota (TRQ) system for imports of wheat, corn, rice, soy oil, cotton, barley and vegetable oils. The quota amounts were not publicly announced, application and allocation procedures were not transparent, and importation occurred through state trading enterprises. China later introduced a TRQ system for fertilizer imports. Under these TRQ systems, China places quantitative restrictions on the amount of these commodities that can enter at a low "in-quota" tariff rate; any imports over that quantity are charged a prohibitively high duty.

As part of its WTO accession commitments, China was to establish large and increasing TRQs for imports of wheat, corn, rice, cotton, wool, sugar, rapeseed oil, palm oil, soybean oil and fertilizer, with most in-quota duties ranging from 1 percent to 9 percent. Each year, a portion of each TRQ is to be reserved for importation through non-state trading entities. China's accession agreement sets forth specific rules for administration of the TRQs, including increased transparency and reallocation of unused quotas to end-users that have an interest in importing. China phased out the vegetable oil TRQs in 2006, but currently maintains a TRQ regime on six agricultural products including wheat, cotton, corn, rice, wool and sugar, as well as three chemical fertilizers including di-ammonium phosphate.

For the first two years after China's WTO accession, China's implementation of its TRQ systems generated numerous complaints from foreign suppliers, with the most serious problems being lack of transparency, sub-divisions of the TRQ, small allocation sizes and burdensome licensing procedures. Repeated engagement by U.S. officials led to regulatory and operational changes by NDRC for shipments beginning January 1, 2004. Key changes included the elimination of separate allocations for general trade and processing trade, the elimination of certain unnecessary licensing requirements, and the creation of a new mechanism for identifying allocation recipients. In 2004, improvements in NDRC's TRQ administration became evident, although transparency continued to be problematic for some of the commodities subject to TRQs.

While NDRC was implementing the systemic changes in 2004, exports of some bulk agricultural commodities from the United States showed substantial increases, largely due to market conditions. In particular, despite some continuing problems with NDRC's handling of the cotton TRQs, U.S. cotton exports totaled a record \$1.4 billion in both 2004 and 2005, followed by a new record of \$2.1

billion in 2006. In addition, U.S. wheat exports totaled $495 million in 2004, as the TRQ allocations for wheat did not appear to act as a limiting factor, but declined significantly to $78 million in 2005 and then to $23 million in 2006. The drop in U.S. wheat exports was due to higher production and lower prices in China, which reduced China's overall import demand.

Meanwhile, the administration of China's TRQ system for fertilizer, handled by SETC and subsequently MOFCOM, has suffered from systemic problems since China's WTO accession. By 2006, this system was still operating with insufficient transparency, and administrative guidance still seemed to be affecting how the allocated quota was used. U.S. fertilizer exports to China have declined throughout the post-WTO accession period, due in part to continuing problems with MOFCOM's administration of the fertilizer TRQ system and in part to increasing subsidization, and resulting overcapacity, of China's domestic fertilizer industry. U.S. fertilizer exports to China decreased from $676 million in 2002 to $355 million in 2005. In 2006, U.S. fertilizer exports to China declined sharply again, totaling $232 million for the year.

In October 2006, perhaps in an attempt by the central authorities to rein in provincial and local efforts to build further unneeded capacity, the Tariff Policy Commission of the State Council announced a temporary reduction of the in-quota tariff rate for fertilizer from 4 percent to 1 percent, effective November 2006. It is too early to tell what effect this change may have on U.S. fertilizer exports to China. However, U.S. and other foreign fertilizer producers were anticipating increased exports after December 11, 2006, when China was scheduled to begin allowing foreign enterprises to engage in the wholesale and retail distribution of fertilizer within China.

Import Licenses

In the early 1990s, China began to reduce substantially the number of products subject to import licensing requirements. With its WTO accession in December 2001, China committed to the fair and nondiscriminatory application of licensing procedures. Among other things, China also committed upon its WTO accession to limit the information that a trader must provide in order to receive a license, in order to ensure that licenses are not unnecessarily burdensome, and to increase transparency and predictability in the licensing process.

MOFTEC issued new regulations and implementing rules to facilitate licensing procedures shortly after China's accession to the WTO. However, license applicants initially reported that they had to provide sensitive business details unnecessary for simple import monitoring. In some sectors, importers also reported that MOFTEC was using a "one-license-per-shipment" system rather than providing licenses to firms for multiple shipments. MOFTEC began to allow more than one shipment per license in late 2002 following U.S. interventions, without modifying the measure authorizing the "one-license-per-shipment" system. In December 2004, MOFCOM issued revised licensing procedures for imported goods. Among other changes, import licenses no longer have quantitative restrictions, provisions related to designated trading were removed, and provisions allowing more than one license per shipment and an "under or over provision" for overloaded or short shipments were added.

China is the world's largest importer of iron ore, accounting for over 40 percent of global iron ore imports (based on 2006 data). Increasing global steel production, led by Chinese growth, has contributed to significant price increases over the past several years. In May 2005, after Chinese steel producers negotiated contracts with major foreign iron ore suppliers, the Chinese government began imposing new import licensing procedures for iron ore without prior WTO notification. Even though the WTO's Import Licensing Agreement calls for import licensing procedures that do not have a restrictive effect on trade, China reportedly restricted licenses to 48 traders and 70 steel producers and has not made public a list of the qualified enterprises or the qualifying criteria used. While the Chinese government maintained that it did not impose any qualifying criteria, it did acknowledge that two organizations affiliated with the Chinese government -- the China Steel Industry Association and the Commercial Chamber for Metals, Minerals and Chemicals Importers and Exporters -- had been discussing a set of rules regarding qualifying criteria such as production capacity and trade performance. In 2006, the United States continued to engage China and monitor developments, as this situation could set a troubling precedent for the handling of imports of other raw materials.

China's inspection and quarantine agency, the State Administration of Quality Supervision, Inspection and Quarantine (AQSIQ), has also imposed inspection-related requirements that have led to restrictions on imports of many U.S. agricultural goods. In particular, two AQSIQ measures issued in 2002 require importers to obtain a Quarantine Inspection Permit (QIP) prior to signing purchase contracts for nearly all traded agricultural commodities. QIPs are one of the most important trade policy issues affecting the United States and China's other agricultural trading partners.

AQSIQ sometimes slows down or even suspends issuance of QIPs at its discretion, without notifying traders in advance or explaining its reasons, resulting in significant commercial uncertainty. Because of the commercial necessity to contract for commodity shipments when prices are low, combined with the inherent delays in having QIPs issued, many cargoes of products such as soybeans, meat and poultry arrive in Chinese ports without QIPs, creating delays in discharge and resulting in demurrage bills for Chinese purchasers. In addition, traders report that shipment are often closely scrutinized and are at risk for disapproval if they are considered too large in quantity.

Some improvements were made to the QIP system in 2004 following repeated U.S. engagement, both bilaterally and at the WTO. In June 2004, AQSIQ issued Decree 73, the Items on Handling the Review and Approval for Entry Animal and Plant Quarantine, which extended the period of validity for QIPs from three months to six months. AQSIQ also began issuing QIPs more frequently within the established time lines. Nevertheless, a great deal of uncertainty remains even with the extended period of validity, because a QIP still locks purchasers into a very narrow period to purchase, transport and discharge cargoes or containers before the QIP's expiration, and because AQSIQ continues to administer the QIP system in a seemingly arbitrary manner.

In 2006, the QIP system saw little improvement, and traders continued to be concerned that the rules and regulations of the QIP system remain available as an administrative tool to limit the quantity of imports. However, traders remain hesitant to press AQSIQ for change because they would risk reprisals. Many of them would at least like AQSIQ to eliminate the quantity requirements that it unofficially places on QIPs. These quantity requirements have been used often by AQSIQ during peak harvest periods to limit the flow of commodity imports. Eliminating this requirement would help to ensure that QIPs do not interfere with the market.

Chapter 3

INTERNAL POLICIES

Taxation

Income Taxes

In April 2001, the National People's Congress passed long-awaited changes to the tax collection law, designed to standardize and increase the transparency of China's tax procedures. The State Council issued detailed regulations for the implementation of this law in September 2002. As part of a broader campaign to "rectify market order" and eliminate inter-provincial barriers to domestic commerce, the Chinese central government also implemented measures to prevent local governments from applying tax treatment that discriminated in favor of locally owned firms.

In order to narrow the widening urban-rural income gap, the Central Committee of the Communist Party of China and the State Council issued Document No. 1 of 2004, which instructed the governments at all levels to reduce the agricultural tax rate of 8.4 percent by 1 percent in 2004, along with the removal of all taxes on special farm produce except for tobacco. Document No. 1 also calls for further reductions in the agricultural tax rate until it is totally eliminated within five years. Where fiscally feasible, local governments were also called upon to reduce or eliminate agricultural taxes more quickly. Agricultural taxes were abolished nationwide effective January 2006.

Foreign investors, including those who have used investment as an entry point to the Chinese domestic market, have benefited from investment incentives such as tax holidays and grace periods, which allow them to reduce substantially their tax burden. Domestic enterprises have long resented rebates and other tax benefits enjoyed by foreign-invested firms, and these benefits may be gradually phased out. According to the tax laws and regulations currently in place, domestic and foreign-invested companies in China are subject to an income tax rate of 33 percent, but because of various tax waivers and incentives most domestic enterprises pay 24 percent and most foreign businesses pay 15 percent.

In December 2006, the Standing Committee of China's National People's Congress conducted its first deliberations over a draft law that proposes to unify corporate income tax rates for domestic and foreign companies in China. The draft law reportedly calls for a universal tax rate of 25 percent, with a 5-year grace period for foreign businesses. The draft law also reportedly includes the following preferential policies: (1) a 20 percent tax rate for small-sized businesses that are marginally profitable; (2) a 15 percent tax rate for government-supported key high technology enterprises; (3) preferential policies to venture capital and investments in environment protection, resource and water conservation and work safety; (4) extension of current preferential tax policies for investment in agriculture, forestry, husbandry, fishery and infrastructure (such as airports, railways and irrigation works); and (5) alternative preferential policies replacing the current preferential policy of awarding direct tax holidays to businesses created for laid off workers and disabled as well as businesses performing resource recycling. Because the draft law has not been circulated publicly, it is not clear whether, or on what timetable, existing preferential export-related policies benefiting foreign-invested enterprises (discussed below in the section on Export Subsidies) would be withdrawn. If the draft law comes into effect, the impact on foreign-invested firms whose businesses have benefited from lower taxes could be significant. Chinese companies, in general, will have a reduced tax burden, making them more competitive with these foreign-invested firms. At the same time, investment in the production of goods with higher technological content and in infrastructure could well rise as a result of the contemplated preferential policies.

Value-Added Taxes

Application of China's single most important revenue source – the VAT, which ranges between 13 percent and 17 percent, depending on the product – continues to be uneven. Importers from a wide range of sectors report that, because taxes on imported goods are reliably collected at the border, they are sometimes subject to application of a VAT that their domestic competitors often fail to pay. As discussed above in the section on Import Substitution Policies, the United States was successful in obtaining China's agreement to remove discriminatory VAT policies favoring domestically-produced semiconductors. In addition, China's selective exemption of certain fertilizer products from the VAT has operated to the disadvantage of imports from the United States.

Meanwhile, China maintains a measure that provides VAT refunds for foreign-invested enterprises when they purchase domestically made equipment, as discussed above in the section on Import Substitution Policies. These refunds are not available for purchases of imported equipment or equipment assembled in China from imported parts. In addition, another measure makes VAT exemptions available to foreign-invested enterprises with regard to imported equipment used to produce their products, provided that they export 100 percent of their production, as discussed below in the section on Export Subsidies.

China retains an active VAT rebate program for exports, although rebate payments are often delayed. In 2003, China announced the reduction of VAT rebates for exports by 3 percentage points, partly in response to foreign complaints about an under-valued renminbi (RMB). Although State Administration of Taxation officials reportedly plan to eliminate rebates eventually in order to increase tax revenues, China has continued this practice in order to spur domestic economic growth. In December 2004, for example, the Ministry of Finance and the State Administration of Taxation issued a circular announcing an increase in the VAT rebate rate from 13 percent to 17 percent for the export of certain information technology products, including integrated circuits, independent components, mobile telecommunication equipment and terminals, computers and periphery equipment, and numerically controlled machine tools. In 2005, China adjusted the ratio of the share of the export VAT refund burden between the central and local governments, from 75-25 to 92.5-7.5. China also halted refunds for some products in high demand domestically in order to discourage their export. For example, China eliminated a 13 percent VAT rebate for exports of steel billets and ingots, although it maintained VAT rebates of 8 percent to 13 percent for more processed steel products. In September 2006, China sought to discourage exports by eliminating VAT rebates for exports of coal, non-ferrous metal and waste and scrap, silicon and certain primary wood products, among other products, and by lowering existing VAT rebates for a variety of steel, non-ferrous metal, textiles and ceramics products.

Meanwhile, China continues to consider fundamental reform of its VAT regime and, in particular, the transformation from a production-based regime to one that is consumption-based. China has pursued a pilot program in the Northeast, but it is unclear when this reform might be extended nationwide.

Consumption Taxes

China's 1993 consumption tax system continues to raise concerns among U.S. exporters. Because China uses a substantially different tax base to compute consumption taxes for domestic and imported products, the tax burden imposed on imported consumer goods ranging from alcoholic beverages to cosmetics to automobiles is higher than for competing domestic products.

Chapter 4

STANDARDS, TESTING, LABELING AND CERTIFICATION

In its WTO accession agreement, China committed to ensure that its regulatory authorities apply the same standards, technical regulations and conformity assessment procedures to both imported and domestic goods and use the same fees, processing periods and complaint procedures for both imported and domestic goods. China also committed that, in order to eliminate unnecessary barriers to trade, it would not maintain multiple or duplicative conformity assessment procedures and would not impose requirements exclusively on imported products. China further committed to ensure that its standards developers, regulatory authorities and conformity assessment bodies operated with transparency and allowed reasonable opportunities for public comment on proposed standards, technical regulations and conformity assessment procedures.

In anticipation of these commitments, China devoted significant energy to reforming its standards and testing and certification regimes prior to its WTO entry. In April 2001, China merged its domestic standards and conformity assessment agency and entry-exit inspection and quarantine agency into one new organization, AQSIQ. Chinese officials explained that this merger was designed to eliminate discriminatory treatment of imports, including requirements for multiple testing simply because a product was imported rather than domestically-produced. China also formed two quasi-independent agencies administratively under AQSIQ: (1) the Certification and Accreditation Administration of China (CNCA), which is charged with the task of unifying, implementing and administering the country's conformity assessment regime; and (2) the Standardization Administration of China (SAC), which is responsible for setting mandatory national standards, unifying China's administration of product standards and aligning its standards and technical regulations with international practices and China's commitments under the WTO Agreement on Technical Barriers to Trade (TBT Agreement).

In January 2002, China began the task of bringing its standards regime more in line with international practice with AQSIQ's issuance of rules designed to facilitate China's adoption of international standards. China subsequently embarked on the task of reviewing all of its existing 21,000 technical regulations to determine their continuing relevance and consistency with international standards. In November 2005, China reported that as of October 2005 it had nullified 1,416 national standards as a result of this review. China has since continued its review of existing standards ands technical regulations, but has not provided an update on its progress.

Nevertheless, in a number of sectors, including automobiles, automotive parts, telecommunications equipment, Internet protocols, wireless local area networks (see the "WAPI" section below), radio frequency identification technology, audio and video coding, food products and consumer products such as cosmetics, concern has grown as China has pursued the development of unique technical requirements, despite the existence of well-established international standards. These China-specific standards, which sometimes appear to lack a sound technical or scientific basis, could create significant barriers to entry into China's markets because of the high cost of compliance for foreign companies.

The lack of transparency in China's standards development process also troubles many foreign companies. The vast majority of Chinese standards-setting bodies are not fully open to foreign participation, in some cases refusing membership to foreign firms and in other cases refusing to allow companies with majority foreign ownership to vote. In some cases, foreign firms are allowed non-voting observer status, but are required to pay membership fees far in excess of those paid by the domestic voting members. Nevertheless, in 2005, some U.S. companies and industry groups concluded that China had begun to make progress in reforming its standardization system by strengthening its links with standards-setters in other countries and by moving its standards regime into closer conformity with international practice.

China's designated notification authority, MOFCOM, has been notifying proposed technical regulations and conformity assessment procedures to WTO Members, as required by the WTO Agreement on Technical Barriers to Trade. Almost all of these notified measures, however, have emanated from AQSIQ or SAC, and few of the trade-related technical regulations drafted by other agencies have been notified. Lack of meaningful comment periods also remains an issue. In many cases, an agency provides insufficient time for the submission of comments, and allots little time for the agency's consideration of those comments, before it finalizes a measure.

Despite China's commitment to apply the same standards and fees to domestic and imported products upon its accession to the WTO, many U.S. industries have complained about China's manipulation of technical regulations and standards to favor domestic industries. In fact, SAC issued a strategy report in September 2004 promoting China's development of standards and technical regulations as a means of protecting domestic industry as tariff rates fall. At the sub-national level, importers have expressed concern that local officials do not understand China's WTO commitments and apply arbitrary technical regulations and standards to protect local industries. These problems are compounded by the fact that coordination between AQSIQ and its affiliated bodies, CNCA and SAC, is lacking, as is coordination between these bodies and China Customs and other ministries and agencies, at both the central and local government levels, on issues related to technical regulations.

China's China Compulsory Certification (CCC) mark system took full effect in August 2003, following a transition period that lasted for fifteen months. The CCC mark replaced the prior "Great Wall" and "CCIB" marks and is now required for more than 130 product categories, such as electrical machinery, information technology equipment, household appliances and their components. In 2006, as in prior years, U.S. companies continued to complain that the regulations lack clarity regarding the products that require a CCC mark. They also have reported that China is applying the CCC mark requirements inconsistently and that many domestic products required by CNCA's regulations to have the CCC mark are still being sold without it. U.S. companies in some sectors also complained that certification remains a difficult, time-consuming and costly process. The process involves on-site inspection of manufacturing facilities outside of China, the cost of which is borne by producers. In addition, small- and medium-sized

U.S. companies without a presence in China find it particularly burdensome to apply for CCC mark exemptions, such as for replacement and re-export, because China requires the applications to be done in person in the Beijing offices of CNCA. China also continues to require the CCC mark for products that would no longer seem to warrant mandatory certification, such as low-risk products and components.

To date, CNCA has accredited well over one hundred Chinese enterprises accreditation to test and certify for purposes of the CCC mark. Despite China's commitment that qualifying minority foreign-owned (upon China's accession to the WTO) and majority foreign-owned (two years later) joint venture conformity assessment bodies would be eligible for accreditation and would be accorded national treatment, China so far has not accredited any foreign-invested conformity assessment bodies. As a result, exporters to China are often required to submit their products to Chinese laboratories for duplicative tests that have already been performed abroad, resulting in greater expense and a longer time to market.

The concerns of U.S. exporters about the CCC mark are heightened by the increasing product scope of the CCC mark certification system. Beginning in 2004, several new categories of products have been added to the list of products requiring the CCC mark, including the addition of six categories of toy products, beginning on June 1, 2007. Additionally, the "China RoHS" scheme discussed below will utilize the CCC mark certification process for certain products to ensure compliance.

In other conformity assessment contexts, some importers report discriminatory treatment and uneven enforcement of technical regulations and standards. For example, foreign companies' products can only be tested in certain designated laboratories. Limited testing and certification capacity means that evaluations sometimes take much longer than international best practice would suggest is appropriate. As testing and certification capacity expands to meet this demand, U.S. companies with multi-country operations worry that inexperienced laboratories might make negative determinations that would have global consequences for the company.

Meanwhile, redundant testing requirements continue to trouble U.S. companies, particularly in cosmetics, new chemicals, pharmaceuticals, medical equipment, cellular telephones and other telecommunications products, consumer electronic products and automobiles. For example, China often requires telecommunications and information technology equipment to be tested and certified to the same electromagnetic compatibility requirements by both MII and CNCA. In December 2004, SAC created technical committees to develop standards for testing environmental equipment, products developed through biotechnology, and new plant and animal varieties, suggesting that foreign companies may soon see additional requirements in these industries as well.

U.S. companies also cite problems with a lack of transparency in the certification process, lack of coordination among standards bodies, burdensome requirements and long processing times for licenses. Some companies have also expressed concern that their intellectual property will be released to competitors when they submit samples of high technology products for mandatory testing. Technical committees that evaluate products for licensing and certification are generally drawn from a pool of government, academic and industrial experts that companies fear may be too closely associated with their competitors. In some cases, laboratories responsible for testing imported products are affiliated with domestic competitors, making the possibility of intellectual property theft more likely.

WAPI

A particularly significant example of China's development of unique technical requirements, despite the existence of well-established international standards, arose in May 2003, when China issued two standards for encryption over Wireless Local Area Networks (WLANs), applicable to domestic and imported equipment containing WLAN (sometimes referred to as Wi-Fi) technologies. Conformance to these standards was scheduled to become mandatory in June 2004. The standards incorporated the WLAN Authentication and Privacy Infrastructure (WAPI) encryption algorithm for secure communications. This component of the standards differed significantly from internationally recognized standards. China sought to enforce the use of WAPI by mandating a particular algorithm (rather than mandating the need for encryption, and leaving the choice of the algorithm to the market) and providing the necessary algorithm only to a limited number of Chinese companies. U.S. and other foreign manufacturers would have been compelled to work with and through these companies, some of which were competitors, and provide them with their proprietary technical product specifications. Following high-level bilateral engagement, China agreed in April 2004 to postpone indefinitely implementation of WAPI and to work within international standards bodies on future development of wireless standards. This commitment led China to submit WAPI for consideration in the International Organization for Standardization (ISO) and International Electrotechnical Commission's (IEC) Joint Technical Committee 1 (ISO/IEC JTC1). In 2006, following balloting of ISO/IEC JTC1 members, the proposed WAPI amendment did not get enough votes to be accepted as an international standard.

In December 2005, the Ministry of Finance (MOF), MII and NDRC jointly issued the Opinions for Implementing Government Procurements of Wireless Local Areas Network. This measure seems to require all government agencies, quasi-government bodies and government-affiliated organizations, when procuring WLAN and related products using fiscal funds, to give priority to WAPI-compliant products. This measure took effect in February 2006. The United States has been monitoring developments in this area, but so far the trade effects of this policy appear to be limited.

Chemical Registration

In September 2003, China's State Environmental Protection Administration (SEPA) issued a regulation requiring manufacturers and importers of new chemicals to apply to SEPA's Chemical Registration Center (CRC) for approval and to provide extensive test data to substantiate the physical properties, consumer safety and environmental impact of the new chemical. U.S. industry's primary concerns are that CRC has not been able to make decisions on the approval of new chemicals in a timely manner and that the governing rules and testing requirements are not transparent and accessible. SEPA's CRC acknowledges receipt of more than 40 completed applications for new chemicals since October 2003. According to the most recent information available from U.S. industry, only a small number of new chemical applications have been approved.

U.S. industry notes that a number of applications have been pending well beyond the 120-day timeline set forth in the regulation. U.S. industry also complains of shifting requirements and implementation changes, such as recently expanded eco-toxicity testing requirements, which mandate that certain eco-toxicity testing, particularly fish eco-toxicity and bio-degradation studies, be carried out in one of six SEPA-accredited laboratories in China. These accredited laboratories have all been established since mid-2004 in response to the September 2003 regulation, and U.S. industry fears that if inexperience leads one of these new laboratories to declare a product unsafe, it could affect sales globally. China's lack of a low-volume exemption, meaning an exemption where trade in a given chemical falls below an annual volume threshold, also appears to hinder the importation of U.S. chemicals, particularly for high-value specialty chemicals sold in small quantities.

Toxic Chemicals

In December 2005, SEPA and the General Administration on Customs issued the Circular on the Highly Restricted Import/Export Toxic Chemicals List five days before it entered into force. In response to U.S. complaints that the notice period was too short, SEPA provided a transition period until June 2006 during which the regulation was apparently not enforced against shipments of chemicals imported from the United States. China subsequently notified the measure to the WTO TBT Committee in June 2006, with no opportunity for comment and no transition period. In addition to these problems, U.S. industry has expressed concerns about excessive fees required to register chemical products, as well as a lack of clarity on the scope of coverage of the measure.

Hazardous Substances

MII and six other Chinese agencies jointly issued the Administrative Measures on the Control of Pollution Caused by Electronic Information Products (China RoHS) in February 2006, with a March 2007 effective date. China did not notify China RoHS to the WTO TBT Committee until May 2006. China had notified an earlier measure setting out the broad framework for China RoHS, the Administrative Measure on Electronic Information Pollution Control, in September 2005, but it provided little detail on how China RoHS would operate.

The objective of China RoHS is to restrict the use of lead, mercury, cadmium, hexavalent chromium, poly-brominated bi-phenyls (PBB) and poly-brominated di-phenyl ethers (PBDE) in certain electrical information products. China RoHS has two main components. One component involves labeling and marking requirements for a long list of electrical information equipment products, which goes into effect in March 2007. The other component involves a planned requirement for in-country testing and certification using China's CCC mark system; however, the effective date for this requirement, and the products to which it will be applicable, remain unclear.

China RoHS is similar to a pre-existing European Union measure (EU RoHS Directive). However, China RoHS differs from the EU RoHS Directive in several ways, including through a different scope of products, unique requirements for labeling and marking across a wide range of electrical information equipment products and a requirement for CCC mark registration to test and certify the absence of the restricted substances in an as yet undetermined catalogue of products.

The China RoHS scheme has created substantial concern for U.S. and other foreign companies in several ways. These companies have expressed concerns about the justification for, and the burdensome nature of, China's labeling and marking requirements for a long list of products. The EU RoHS regulations do not require labeling. Additionally, the issue of how China's labeling and marking requirements will be applied to products containing many electrical information product components has not been adequately addressed by Chinese regulators, nor have the mandated labeling and marking requirements been notified to the WTO TBT Committee for review and comment.

Companies have also expressed concern about China's plans to require an in-country testing and certification process using the CCC mark system for the as yet to be determined catalogue of products that will be banned if they contain the hazardous substances identified above. No other country regulating hazardous substances in electrical information products requires in-country, government-administered testing for compliance, according to U.S. industry. For example, the

EU requires companies to self-declare their conformity with the EU RoHS Directive.

Scrap Recycling

Scrap exports from the United States to China exceeded $4 billion in 2006, making scrap one of the United States' largest exports to China by value. In late 2003, China's AQSIQ issued a notice requiring overseas scrap material exporters to register with AQSIQ. The stated purpose of the new requirement was to better monitor the entry of scrap shipments into China reportedly due to high occurrences of receiving dangerous waste and illegal material in past shipments from overseas. It was not until May 2004 that AQSIQ issued the implementing rules. These rules established registration procedures, including an application deadline of July 2004, and set substantive requirements. In response to U.S. and other WTO Members' concerns that the application period was too short, AQSIQ extended the application deadline to August 2004, allowed companies who submitted incomplete applications to supplement required documents and extended the new requirement's effective date from November 2004 to January 2005.

In 2004, AQSIQ made public on its website the names of overseas exporters approved to ship scrap to China in two postings, the first in mid-October and the second at the end of December, only days before the new registration would take effect. In total, about 85 percent of worldwide applicants were granted approval, including hundreds of U.S. exporters. AQSIQ indicated that it would notify applicants that were not approved and that these exporters would be able to apply again six months after receiving notice of their rejection.

In July 2005, AQSIQ posted Bulletin No. 103/2005 on its website, announcing the resumption of the review and approval of registration applications for scrap imports. According to the bulletin, as of August 2005, scrap suppliers must wait three years to reapply for registration if they are denied eligibility. A December 2005 AQSIQ notice reported that an additional 260 company registrations had been approved, including 55 U.S. companies.

Since Bulletin No. 103/2005 was published, U.S. scrap exporters continue to experience problems related to inconsistent and unexplained rejections of licenses, confusing requirements imposed with little or no notice, and rejections of shipments at the point of entry. Problems are also being encountered within the United States as a result of pre-inspection requirements imposed by the Chinese authorities and conducted by Chinese-authorized inspectors at the shipment origin point.

Scrap Waste

In December 2004, China's President Hu Jintao signed Presidential Order No. 31, publishing the amended Law for the Prevention of Solid Scrap Waste Pollution, which went into effect in April 2005. According to this law, firms manufacturing, selling and importing items listed in the mandatory reclamation catalogue must recycle these items, and it is illegal to import scrap waste as component materials that cannot be rendered safe. Depending on the particular item, items that can be safely used as component materials are subject to either restricted import procedures or automatic licensing procedures. SEPA is charged with coordinating with MOFCOM, NDRC, China Customs and AQSIQ to design, adjust and publish the catalogues of imported solid scrap waste subject to the restricted or automatic licensing regimes. SEPA and MOFCOM, meanwhile, are responsible for reviewing and issuing licenses for the items subject to restricted import procedures.

Medical Devices

China still requires outdated type-testing (batch testing) for medical devices. Quality systems audits, a common practice in other major markets, address product safety and efficacy in a more rigorous manner than type-testing. As a result, requiring firms that have undergone internationally recognized quality systems audits to also be type-tested is redundant and does not provide any additional safety benefits, while it adds unnecessary costs and delays in getting needed medical device products to Chinese patients. Certain electro-medical devices also face redundant testing by two different agencies, the State Food and Drug Administration (SFDA) and AQSIQ, which administers the "CCC" mark for electrical safety. Both agencies perform virtually identical product tests and factory inspections prior to registration, but they do not recognize the results of one another's tests and inspections. The U.S. medical devices industry reports that this redundancy adds significant time and costs to bringing a new technology to market in China without providing any additional safety benefits.

At the April 2006 JCCT meeting, China committed to eliminate the testing and certification redundancies in the medical devices sector. However, AQSIQ/SFDA Notice No. 70, issued in April 2006, intended by China to fulfill the JCCT commitment, only eliminated a single redundancy. It only eliminated redundant testing and redundant testing fees, while failing to address separate and redundant AQSIQ and SFDA application fees, certification processes and inspection teams for inspecting the manufacturing facilities of medical device makers in the United States and other countries.

A similar concern exists for imported pacemakers, which are inspected by AQSIQ after clearing customs. This review adds unnecessary delay and costs to the distribution of these pacemakers, without providing any additional safety benefits, as pacemakers are scanned and re-calibrated by the hospital before implantation into patients.

Sanitary and Phytosanitary (SPS) Measures

In 2006, China's general lack of transparency remained a problem. China either failed to notify or belatedly notified to the WTO numerous SPS measures, resulting in measures that were adopted without the benefit of comments from other interested WTO Members. In addition, in some cases, the adopted measures were overly burdensome, appeared to lack a scientific foundation, or raised significant national treatment concerns. U.S. engagement with China at the WTO and bilaterally, including through the provision of technical assistance, has helped to ensure China's compliance with certain WTO transparency obligations. At the same time, however, various U.S. agricultural exports continued to be subjected to unnotified entry, inspection and labeling requirements or faced unwarranted import bans. The most problematic of China's SPS measures are described below.

Bovine Spongiform Encephalopathy (BSE)-Related Bans on Beef and Low-Risk Bovine Products

In December 2003, China and other countries imposed a ban on U.S. cattle, beef and processed beef products in response to a case of BSE found in a dairy cow which had been imported from Canada into the United States. Since that time, the United States has repeatedly provided China with extensive technical information on all aspects of its BSE-related surveillance and mitigation measures, internationally recognized by the World Organization for Animal Health (OIE) as effective and appropriate, for both food safety and animal health.

After three years, China still has not provided any scientific justification for continuing to maintain its ban, nor has it identified any of the administrative and regulatory steps necessary to lift the ban. Although China finally sent a technical team to the United States in October 2005, this visit did not advance a resolution of the impasse. At the April 2006 JCCT meeting, China agreed to conditionally reopen the Chinese market to U.S. beef, subject to the negotiation and finalization of an import protocol by technical experts on an expedited basis. Jointly negotiated protocols, and accompanying export certificates, are normal measures necessary for the export of any livestock products from the United States to China or other trading partners. At the end of June 2006, after three inconclusive rounds of negotiations, China's food safety regulators unilaterally announced a limited market opening, restricted to the entry of U.S. boneless beef from animals 30 months of age or less. One month later, they followed up that announcement with an announcement of 22 onerous entry conditions, many of which were unrelated to BSE. These unilateral announcements had no practical effect, because, as with any trading partners seeking to engage in livestock trade, the United States and China would have had to agree on language for actual export safety certificates before the trade could resume. Since then, the United States has pressed China to reconsider its position and to negotiate an appropriate protocol in light of China's WTO SPS Agreement obligations and relevant OIE guidelines.

At the same time that it banned U.S. cattle, beef and processed beef products, China also banned low-risk or "safe to trade" bovine products (i.e.: bovine semen and embryos, protein-free tallow and non-ruminant feeds and fats) even though they are deemed tradable based on OIE guidelines regardless of a country's BSE status. After numerous bilateral meetings and technical discussions in 2004, including a visit to U.S. bovine facilities by Chinese food safety officials, China announced a lifting of its BSE-related ban for low-risk bovine products in late September 2004. However, China conditioned the lifting of the ban on the negotiation of protocol agreements setting technical and certification parameters for incoming low-risk bovine products. In November 2004, U.S. and Chinese officials finalized and signed protocols that would enable the resumption of exports of U.S.-origin bovine semen and embryos, contingent on facility certification by China's regulatory authorities, as well as a resumption of exports of U.S.-origin non-ruminant feeds and fats. In July 2005, China finally announced the resumption of trade in bovine semen and embryos, following certifications for 52 U.S. facilities made earlier in the year. However, trade in U.S.-origin non-ruminant feeds and fats did not resume, as China's regulatory authorities insisted on a series of onerous, detailed and unnecessary information requirements that are not consistent with OIE guidelines and contrast sharply with U.S. requirements. As a result of further negotiations in December 2005, export certificates were finalized, and trade resumed in early 2006. Meanwhile, trade in protein-free tallow had not resumed by the end of 2006, as U.S. and Chinese officials had not reached agreement on provisions of a protocol.

Avian Influenza (AI)

In February 2004, China imposed a nationwide ban on U.S. poultry in response to cases of low-pathogenic AI found in Delaware. Throughout 2004, the United States provided technical information to China on the U.S. AI situation, and in August 2004 a high-level Chinese delegation conducted a review of the status of AI eradication efforts in the United States. In December 2004, China lifted its nationwide ban on U.S. poultry, leaving in place a ban only for the states of Connecticut and Rhode Island. In early 2005, following the announcement of low-pathogenic AI found in the state of New York, China did not impose a nationwide ban. Instead, demonstrating progress in following OIE guidelines, China imposed a ban limited to poultry from the state of New York.

In 2006, China imposed an import ban on poultry and poultry products originating from the state of Pennsylvania, based on incidents of low-pathogenic AI. China also suspended the importation of heat-treated and cooked poultry and poultry products at the same time, even though the OIE's AI chapter makes clear that products that have been heat-treated in a manner to inactivate the virus should not be subject to an AI-related import ban. Despite China's progress in imposing limited bans, as opposed to nationwide bans, in response to cases of AI, China's actions are problematic because any ban in response to cases of low-pathogen AI is inconsistent with international standards. The United States is attempting to work with China's regulators to address these issues.

Wheat

The 1999 U.S.-China Agricultural Cooperation Agreement established an agreed level of TCK fungus tolerance in U.S. wheat, and China no longer routinely blocks U.S. wheat exports from the Pacific Northwest on the basis of the TCK fungus. Nevertheless, China has imposed a maximum residue level (MRL) for selenium that is more stringent than the international standard and threatens U.S. wheat exports to China. In addition, China has imposed an MRL for vomitoxin in wheat in the absence of any international standard or scientific justification. Although these measures are problematic, U.S. exports of wheat to China appear to be unaffected by them. A drop in U.S. wheat exports in 2006 was attributable to other factors.

Zero Tolerance for Pathogens

Since 2002, China has applied SPS-related requirements on imported raw meat and poultry that do not appear to be consistent with Codex Alimentarius (Codex) guidelines or current scientific testing practices. One requirement establishes a zero tolerance limit for the presence of Salmonella bacteria. A similar zero tolerance standard exist for E. Coli and Listeria pathogens. Meanwhile, the complete elimination of these enteropathogenic bacteria is generally considered unachievable without first subjecting raw meat and poultry to a process of irradiation. Moreover, China apparently does not apply this same standard to domestic raw poultry and meat, raising national treatment concerns.

In late 2005 and early 2006, 14 U.S. pork and poultry plants were de-listed by China for alleged violations of zero tolerance standards for pathogens or detection of certain chemical residues. Despite positive results from USDA Food Safety and Inspection Service investigations of the plants, the majority of the plants were not re-listed as approved to ship products to China until April 2006, following extensive engagement between U.S. and Chinese regulatory officials because of differences between Codex guidelines and China's SPS related requirements on imported raw meat and poultry. Two U.S. plants remain de-listed while U.S. regulatory officials continue to press Chinese regulatory officials to re-list the plants or to provide scientific justification.

Meanwhile, China continues to maintain maximum residue levels (MRLs) for certain heavy metals, veterinary drugs and other residues that are inconsistent with Codex and other international standards. China also enforces a zero tolerance standard for some residues, even where Codex has adopted guidelines that many of China's major trading partners have adopted. U.S. regulatory officials have encouraged their Chinese counterparts to adopt MRLs that are scientifically based, safe and minimally trade disrupting.

Distilled Spirits

Until August 2006, China maintained a mandatory standard on distilled spirits that set maximum limits on naturally occurring substances, known as superior alcohols or fusel oils, which result from the production process. However, the Joint UN FAO/WHO Expert Committee on Food Additives, like U.S. regulators of alcohol, has recognized that superior alcohols are safe for human consumption. In August 2006, after several years of bilateral engagement and interventions by the United States at WTO TBT Committee meetings, China notified a proposed revision of its distilled spirits standard and indicated that it was accepting public comment. According to China's notification, the proposed revision would eliminate the requirement for tolerance levels of superior alcohols, or fusel oil. If adopted, it would bring China's standard in line with international norms.

Food Additive Standards

Another problematic area involves China's overly restrictive food additive standards. China continues to block many U.S. processed food products from entering the Chinese market by banning certain food additives that are widely used in other countries and have been approved by the World Health Organization. The most recent example is China's proposed *Hygienic Standard for Uses of Food Additives*, notified to the WTO in July 2005 so that WTO Members could comment on it. This proposed technical regulation is 237 pages long and covers dozens of residues and additives for nearly 1,000 commodities. In some cases, it employs domestic nomenclature rather than internationally recognized technical terms, making it difficult to assess the impact that it would have on specific products. The United States recently submitted detailed comments on the proposed technical regulation and asked China to delay its adoption until a thorough review could take place.

Biotechnology Regulations

In January 2002, the Ministry of Agriculture (MOA) issued new rules implementing June 2001 regulations on agricultural biotechnology safety, testing and labeling. The product most affected by these rules was soybeans, while corn and other commodities were also potentially affected. However, the rules did not provide adequate time for completion of required safety assessments before their effective date of March 20, 2002. In response to U.S. interventions, China issued interim rules, which allowed trade to continue while authorities carried out safety assessments of biotechnology products. These interim rules were extended twice and were set to expire in April 2004. In December 2003 talks, MOA officials promised that approval of Round-up Ready soybeans would be completed at least 60 days before expiration of the interim rules in order to prevent any trade disruption. China followed through on this promise and approved Round-up Ready soybeans, along with two cotton events and two corn events, in February 2004. Two months later, China issued final safety certificates for four additional corn events and seven canola events. China issued a formal safety certificate for another corn event later in 2004, leaving only one corn event still awaiting final approval. During the July 2005 JCCT meeting, MOA issued the final safety certificate for the remaining corn event. All of the approvals made in 2004 and 2005 were for three-year renewable safety certificates. In January 2007, MOA renewed safety certificates for all of the events that had originally been approved three years earlier.

Other U.S. concerns with China's biotechnology regulations remain. Areas of concern include limited timelines for submission of products, lack of clarity on assessment requirements for stacked (multiple trait) products and, at times, duplicative and unprecedented testing requirements.

Food Labeling

The U.S. processed food industry has registered concerns with a number of standards and labeling requirements on its exports to China. The meat industry in particular is concerned that labeling regulations issued in late 2002 contain several requirements that go beyond those of any other country. It asserts that these requirements are unnecessary and costly.

Chinese agricultural importers and importers of processed foods are also concerned about measures requiring labels for products containing material developed through the use of biotechnology, such as soybeans and corn. The June 2001 biotechnology regulations issued by MOA require labeling of bulk commodities, but implementation has been limited and sporadic. Future implementation of these measures remains uncertain.

The distilled spirits industry is concerned that China will require its products to comply with all existing food labeling requirements. The industry believes that some of these requirements are inappropriate. For example, China requires distilled spirits product labels to include a bottling date. According to accepted international practice relating to wines and spirits, however, the date of manufacture (production or bottling date) is not required. Because many spirits products consist of a blend of spirits that are aged for varying periods, a single "date of manufacture" is often not possible to specify, would not represent the actual age of the product and would confuse consumers regarding the actual age of the product. China also requires the labels of distilled spirits products to include a list of ingredients, even though the original ingredients (e.g., corn, wheat, rye and barley) are completely transformed and are no longer present after distillation. Furthermore, China maintains typeface specifications and translation requirements that are inconsistent with international standards.

Chapter 5

EXPORT REGULATION

Export Licenses and Quotas

Over the last several years, China has progressively reduced the number of products requiring some type of export license. In 2005, China continued this trend, as it freed up three additional categories of products from this requirement (man-made jade, satin and some kinds of silk). As of the end of 2006, China continued to maintain export licensing requirements for 46 categories of products (totaling 312 items at the 8-digit tariff level), including important industrial raw materials like coke, fluorspar and rare earth oxides, as well as certain grains, cotton, livestock, certain metals, lethal chemicals and food products. In addition, China occasionally imposes new export licensing requirements on strategically sensitive commodities.

For some products, such as coke (a key steel input) and fluorspar (a key ingredient in a wide range of downstream products made with fluorocarbons), the export licensing system raises serious concerns under WTO rules that generally prohibit export restrictions. Export licenses for these two products are accompanied by export quotas and at times have required the payment of high export license fees beyond the administrative costs of administering an export license system.

In 2004, China's export restrictions on coke began to have a significant, adverse effect on U.S. integrated steel producers and their customers, as China's increasingly restrictive export restrictions pushed the export price of Chinese coke to the vicinity of $500 per metric ton (MT), more than three times the price in 2003. After a series of meetings in which the United States urged China to eliminate the practice of using export restrictions, not just for coke but also for other products, China raised the 2004 quota allotment for coke to 12.3 million MT, and it indicated that it would eventually raise the quota to the 2003 level of 14.3 million MT. Shortly thereafter, MOFCOM also issued an urgent notice reiterating that the sale of export licenses was illegal. In the ensuing months, with the increased supply of Chinese coke and the crackdown on the sale of export licenses, the export prices for Chinese coke declined significantly.

U.S. industry was also able to obtain a substantially larger quantity of Chinese coke in 2004 than it had in 2003.

In May 2005, consistent with earlier indications from China, an NDRC official stated publicly that China would eliminate the coke export quota system as of January 1, 2006. A MOFCOM official also noted that while WTO rules allow Member countries to impose quotas on exports under certain circumstances, the rules simultaneously require restrictions on domestic consumption, which had not been done to date. In November 2005, when MOFCOM announced the 2006 export quota levels for agricultural, industrial and textile products, coke was absent from the list. MOFCOM later indicated that coke would still be subject to an export quota, except the export quota would now be administered by the NDRC, not MOFCOM. The reason given for the switch in coke export quota administration is that NDRC is responsible for dealing with industrial products that have significant influence on the national economy. In early December 2005, the NDRC released a list of 2006 coal export quotas, but did not include coke. In late December 2005, the NDRC finally issued the coke export quota, set at 14 million MT for 2006.

In 2006, even though the export price for Chinese coke remained relatively low compared to the $500 per MT price of 2004, the export quota kept world coke prices artificially high in 2006, and a significant differential existed between China's domestic coke prices and world coke prices. However, the Chinese government continued its efforts to direct market outcomes by maintaining the export quota on coke for 2007. In addition, in October 2006, China took the additional step of imposing a 5 percent duty on exports of coke.

In October 2006, China announced new export duties on certain steel inputs and semi-processed steel products. Applied in combination with differential VAT rebate policies, these export duties act to restrict exports of raw materials and semi-processed inputs (including coke) while promoting the production and export of more processed steel products.

China has imposed quotas and high license fees on exports of fluorspar since before its accession to the WTO, apparently with the objective of supporting China's downstream producers of the numerous products derived from fluorspar, such as non-ozone depleting hydrofluorocarbon refrigerants and foam blowing agents. While their foreign competitors pay higher world market prices for fluorspar, China's downstream producers benefit from the artificially low domestic prices for fluorspar and are able to export their products around the world at prices well below those of their foreign competitors. China has refused to modify its practices in this area, despite repeated U.S. requests. In fact, China has increased the protection afforded to its downstream producers by lowering the export quota on fluorspar each year and, in October 2006, by imposing a 10 percent duty on exports of fluorspar.

In December 2004, China announced plans to impose export duties on certain categories of textile and apparel products in an apparent effort to manage the export growth of textile and apparel products in response to concerns raised by its trading partners as the January 1, 2005 deadline for removal of global textile quotas drew near. In February 2005, MOFCOM issued rules imposing automatic licensing requirements for textile exports to the United States, the European Union and Hong Kong. Subsequently, China suspended the licensing requirements only to restore similar measures in June 2005 and July 2005 after the United States imposed safeguards on certain categories of textile imports from China. China claimed the measures were needed to avoid uncertainty among Chinese textile exporting firms, to encourage exports of high value-added items and to avoid rent seeking in license distributions. Under the June 2005 measures, MOFCOM, China Customs and AQSIQ jointly issued and made adjustments to a catalogue of subject items, listed by tariff codes, destination countries and regions, implementing periods and total licensed export quantities of subject items. Included in the catalogue were textile products subject to foreign safeguard actions or those subject to temporary quantitative regulation in accordance with bilateral agreements. In November 2005, USTR and MOFCOM signed a memorandum of understanding (MOU), under which China agreed to limit export growth rates in 34 categories of textiles, representing approximately 40 percent of bilateral trade in textiles, through 2008. The United States in turn agreed to dismiss all pending China-specific textile safeguard investigations and agreed to exercise restraint in invoking safeguards for categories of textiles falling outside the MOU. The United States and China also established an Electronic Visa Information System Arrangement to monitor trade in the affected products.

China requires export licenses on products that are the subject of antidumping duties in a foreign market. As was initially the case in 2005 for textile exports subject to safeguard limitations in the United States, the central government has often delegated responsibility for issuing these licenses to quasi-governmental industry associations formed to take the place of the ministries that governed production during the earlier central planning era. Foreign investors report that the industry associations are using the power to issue export licenses to force companies to participate in association-supported activities. For example, the steel producers' industry association will not issue an export license to any company that does not contribute to its antidumping defense funds.

Export Subsidies

China officially abolished subsidies in the form of direct budgetary outlays for exports of industrial goods on January 1, 1991. In its WTO accession agreement, China committed to eliminate all subsidies prohibited under Article 3 of the WTO Agreement on Subsidies and Countervailing Measures, including all forms of export subsidies on industrial and agricultural goods, upon its accession to the WTO in December 2001.

A general lack of transparency makes it difficult to identify and quantify possible export subsidies provided by the Chinese government. China's subsidy programs are often the result of internal administrative measures and are not publicized. Sometimes they take the form of income tax reductions or exemptions. They can also take a variety of other forms, including mechanisms such as credit allocations, low-interest loans, debt forgiveness and reduction of freight charges. U.S. industry has alleged that subsidization is a key reason that Chinese exports are undercutting prices in the United States and gaining market share. Of particular concern are China's practices in the steel, petrochemical, high technology, forestry and paper products, textiles, hardwood plywood, machinery and copper and other non-ferrous metals industries.

In April 2006, China finally submitted its long-overdue subsidies notification to the WTO's Subsidies Committee. Although the notification is lengthy, with over 70 subsidy programs reported, it is also notably incomplete, as it failed to notify any subsidies provided by China's state-owned banks or by provincial and local government authorities. In addition, while China notified several subsidies that appear to be prohibited under WTO rules, it did so without making any commitment to withdraw them, and it failed to notify other subsidies that appear to be prohibited.

Through the remainder of 2006, the United States pressed China to withdraw the subsidies that appear to be prohibited, which include both export subsidies and import substitution subsidies and benefit a wide range of industries in China, principally through income tax and VAT exemptions and reductions. However, China was unwilling to commit to the immediate withdrawal of these subsidies.

Accordingly, the United States initiated a challenge to these subsidies under the WTO's dispute settlement procedures in early 2007.

Shortly after China acceded to the WTO, U.S. corn exporters began to complain that China was subsidizing its corn exports. In 2002 and 2003, it appeared that significant quantities of corn had been exported from China, including corn from Chinese government stocks, at prices that may have been 15 percent to 20 percent below domestic prices in China. As a result, U.S. corn exporters were losing market share for corn in their traditional Asian markets, such as South Korea and Malaysia, while China was exporting record amounts of corn. In 2004, however, trade analysts began to conclude that, because of several economic factors, including changes in the relationship between domestic prices and world prices, China was trending toward becoming a net importer of corn. One result appears to be that China's exports are largely made on a commercial basis, although concern remains regarding the operation of China's VAT rebate system for corn.

Chapter 6

INTELLECTUAL PROPERTY RIGHTS (IPR) PROTECTION

With its acceptance of the TRIPS Agreement, China took on obligations to adhere to generally accepted international norms to protect and enforce the intellectual property rights held by U.S. and other foreign companies and individuals in China. Specifically, the TRIPS Agreement sets minimum standards of protection for copyrights and neighboring rights, trademarks, geographical indications, industrial designs, patents, integrated circuit layout designs and undisclosed information. Minimum standards are also established by the TRIPS Agreement for IPR enforcement procedures and remedies. The TRIPS Agreement additionally requires that, with very limited exceptions, WTO Members provide national and most favored nation (MFN) treatment to the nationals of other WTO Members with regard to the protection and enforcement of intellectual property rights.

Since its accession to the WTO, China has overhauled its legal regime and put in place a comprehensive set of laws and regulations aimed at protecting the intellectual property rights of domestic and foreign entities in China. At the same time, some key improvements in China's legal framework are still needed, and China has continued to demonstrate little success in actually enforcing its laws and regulations in the face of the challenges created by widespread counterfeiting, piracy and other forms of infringement. Indeed, USTR's April 2006 report under the Special 301 provisions of U.S. trade law cited inadequate IPR enforcement as one of China's greatest shortcomings as a trading partner. As a result, in 2006, the United States' bilateral engagement with China continued to focus on obtaining improvements to multiple aspects of China's system of IPR protection and enforcement so that significant reductions in IPR infringement in China could be realized and sustained over time.

Several factors contribute to China's poor IPR enforcement record. One major factor is China's chronic underutilization of deterrent criminal remedies. For example, legal measures in China that establish high thresholds for criminal investigation, prosecution and conviction preclude criminal remedies in many instances of commercial-scale counterfeiting and piracy, creating a "safe harbor" for infringers and raising concerns among the United States and some of its major trading partners relating to China's obligations under Article 61 of the TRIPS Agreement. With criminal remedies circumscribed, China's enforcement authorities rely instead on toothless administrative enforcement, which primarily results in small fines, administrative injunctions and other minor inconveniences for infringers. Meanwhile, procedures in civil actions are frequently cumbersome, and civil damages are generally low.

Another exacerbating factor – which also raises WTO concerns – is China's continued maintenance of import restrictions and restrictions on wholesale and retail distribution that reduce and delay market access for certain types of legitimate foreign products, such as movies, video games and books. These restrictions inadvertently help to ensure that infringing products continue to dominate those sectors within China.

China's leaders began to demonstrate a willingness to address U.S. concerns in October 2003, when a new IPR Leading Group was formed, signaling a more focused and sustained effort by China to tackle the IPR enforcement problem. Many officials in China, led by President Hu Jintao, Premier Wen Jiabao and Vice Premier Wu Yi, continued to give voice to China's commitment to protecting intellectual property rights in 2006 and worked hard to make it a reality, as they attempted to improve not only public awareness but also training and coordination among the numerous Chinese government entities involved in IPR enforcement while simultaneously fighting local protectionism and corruption. Sustained involvement by China's leaders is critical if China is to deliver on the IPR commitments that it made at the April 2004, July 2005 and April 2006 JCCT meetings, including China's core commitment to significantly reduce IPR infringement levels across the country.

Building on earlier engagement with China, the United States conducted an out-of-cycle review under the Special 301 provisions of U.S. trade law in 2004 and 2005. This review involved a systematic evaluation of China's entire IPR enforcement regime and concluded in April 2005 with the Administration's elevation of China to the Special 301 "Priority Watch" list and the creation of a comprehensive strategy for addressing China's ineffective IPR enforcement regime, which included the possible use of WTO mechanisms, as appropriate.

Pursuing this new strategy at the July 2005 JCCT meeting, the United States sought and obtained China's agreement to take a series of specific actions designed to: (1) increase criminal prosecutions of IPR violators; (2) improve border enforcement and reduce exports of infringing goods; (3) counter piracy of movies, audio visual products and software; (4) address Internet-related piracy; and (5) assist small- and medium-sized U.S. companies experiencing China-related IPR problems, among other things. To date, China has taken steps to fulfill many of these commitments. It adopted amended rules governing the transfer of administrative and customs cases to criminal authorities, and it took some steps to pursue administrative actions against end-user software piracy. China posted an IPR Ombudsman to its Embassy in Washington, who has facilitated contacts between U.S. Government officials and their counterparts in Beijing, and has been a source of information for U.S. businesses, including small- and medium-sized companies. China has also sought to expand enforcement cooperation.

In October 2005, the United States submitted a request to China under Article 63.3 of the TRIPS Agreement, as did both Japan and Switzerland, seeking more transparency on IPR infringement levels and enforcement activities in China, with the objective of obtaining a better basis for assessing the effectiveness of China's efforts to improve IPR enforcement since China's accession to the WTO.

However, despite the United States' extensive efforts to follow up on its Article 63.3 request bilaterally, China has since provided only limited information in response, hampering the United States' ability to evaluate whether China is taking all necessary steps to address the rampant IPR infringement found throughout China.

In 2006, the United States again used the JCCT process, including the IPR Working Group created at the April 2004 JCCT meeting, to secure new IPR commitments and, in a few instances, specific actions to implement past commitments. During the run-up to the April 2006 JCCT meeting, China took enforcement actions against plants that produce pirated optical discs, and it also issued new rules that require computers to be pre-installed with licensed operating system software. At the meeting itself, China further committed to ensure the legalization of software used in Chinese enterprises and to take up issues of government and enterprise software asset management in the JCCT IPR Working Group. China also agreed to work on cooperation to combat infringing goods displayed at trade fairs in China and to intensify efforts to eliminate infringing products at major consumer markets in China, such as the Silk Street Market in Beijing. The two sides further agreed that they would increase cooperation between their respective law enforcement authorities and customs authorities and that the United States would provide China with additional technical assistance to aid China in fully implementing the WIPO Internet treaties (i.e.: the WIPO Copyright Treaty and the WIPO Performance and Phonograms Treaty). In addition, China reaffirmed its prior commitments to continue efforts to ensure the use of legalized software at all levels of government and to adopt procedures to ensure that enterprises use legal software, beginning with state-owned enterprises and other large enterprises.

To date, China has made some progress in implementing its April 2006 JCCT commitments, but it has been slower than in the past. One bright spot appears to be China's implementation of the new rules requiring computers to be pre-installed with licensed operating system software, as U.S. industry has been pleased with the initial results of that effort.

Legal Framework

In most respects, China's framework of laws, regulations and implementing rules remains largely satisfactory. However, reforms are needed in a few key areas, including certain aspects of the Criminal Law and rapidly emerging fields, such as Internet copyright protection. In particular, right holders have pointed to a number of continuing deficiencies in China's criminal measures. For example, it appears that China would need to eliminate thresholds for criminal prosecution that provide a legal "safe harbor" for many commercial infringers if it is to bring its legal framework into compliance with its TRIPS Agreement obligations. In addition, while China introduced new regulations in 2006 that represent a positive step toward meeting the requirements of the WIPO Internet treaties, more work is needed at both the national level and the provincial level to meet the challenges of Internet piracy and fully implement the WIPO Internet treaties.

At the time of its accession to the WTO, China was in the process of modifying the full range of IPR laws, regulations and implementing rules, including those relating to patents, trademarks and copyrights. China had completed amendments to its Patent Law, Trademark Law and Copyright Law, along with regulations for the Patent Law. Within several months of its accession, China issued regulations for the Trademark Law and the Copyright Law, followed by implementing rules. China also issued regulations and implementing rules covering specific subject areas, such as integrated circuits, computer software and pharmaceuticals. U.S. experts carefully reviewed these measures after their issuance and, together with other WTO Members, participated in a comprehensive review of them before the WTO's TRIPS Council in 2002.

Since 2003, China has periodically issued new IPR laws, regulations and other measures. The U.S. Government has reviewed these measures through bilateral discussions and subsequent TRIPS Council reviews. Encouragingly, China has also become more willing to circulate proposed measures for public comment and to discuss proposed measures with interested trading partners and stakeholders.

In 2006, China announced a new Action Plan for revising its legal regime in order to better protect intellectual property rights. Among other things, this Action Plan sets out China's intentions for revising the Patent Law, the Trademark Law and related measures, and China subsequently did release new versions of both the Patent Law and the Trademark Law for public comment. Since then, the United States has been assessing the potential ramifications of the contemplated revisions for U.S. right holders. The U.S. Government and U.S. industry groups have also submitted written comments, along with invitations to continue dialogue on these important pieces of legislation.

China has also been working on other proposed legal measures that could have significant implications for the intellectual property rights of foreign right holders. In particular, China is drafting an Anti-Monopoly Law and has considered rules relating to the treatment of IPR by standards-setting organizations. The United States is carefully monitoring both of these efforts and has raised concerns with particular aspects of these proposals, both in bilateral meetings and at the WTO.

The United States, meanwhile, has repeatedly urged China to pursue additional legislative and regulatory changes, using both bilateral meetings and the annual transitional reviews before the WTO's TRIPS Council. The focus of U.S. efforts is to persuade China to improve its legal regime in certain critical areas, such as criminal IPR enforcement and legislative and regulatory reform, especially with regard to China's high criminal thresholds and other obstacles to effective enforcement. Other obstacles in the area of criminal enforcement include, for example, the lack of criminal liability for certain acts of copyright infringement, the profit motive requirement in copyright cases, the requirement of identical trademarks in counterfeiting cases and the absence of minimum, proportionate sentences and clear standards for initiation of police investigations in cases where there is a reasonable suspicion of criminal activity. At the same time, the United States has also been pressing China for a variety of changes to its administrative and civil enforcement regimes, such as the restoration of minimum (and deterrent) fines in administrative trademark enforcement cases, increased referral of administrative enforcement actions for criminal prosecution, elimination of the need for legalization and consularization of foreign evidence, implementation of a discovery process with compulsory measures for evidence protection, provision of meaningful injunctive relief and enforcement of judicial orders. While some of these issues do not raise specific WTO concerns, all of them will continue to detract from China's enforcement efforts until addressed.

In its 2006 Action Plan, China did not embrace reform of the Criminal Law, although it did undertake to "improve" its December 2004 judicial interpretation on the handling of criminal IPR cases. Improvement of that measure could include, for example, clarification of some issues related to China's problematic thresholds, but Chinese government officials have given no indication that this process will lead to the reduction or elimination of these thresholds – a key concern for U.S. right holders, particularly in light of China's obligations under Article 61 of the TRIPS Agreement. In the United States' view, China's high thresholds for criminal prosecution help to explain why criminal remedies are so underutilized in China, as these thresholds create a substantial "safe harbor" for commercial-scale infringers. The United States is determined to resolve this problem and, in November 2006, informed China that it would be filing a formal request for WTO consultations on this issue and certain other IPR enforcement issues. However, China asked the United States to delay that filing so that further bilateral discussions could take place. With the support of U.S. industry, the United States agreed to hold further bilateral discussions, with the objective of seeking a resolution in the near term.

The United States has also sought improvements in China's copyright protection in the context of electronic information networks since the April 2004 JCCT meeting. China took an important step at the time of that meeting when the National Copyright Administration (NCA) issued the Measures for Administrative Protection of Copyright on the Internet. That measure requires Internet service providers to take remedial actions to delete content that infringes on copyrights upon receipt of a complaint from the right holder, or face administrative penalties ranging from confiscation of illegal gains to fines of up to RMB100,000 ($12,500).

During the run-up to the July 2005 JCCT meeting, the United States also urged China to accede to the WIPO Internet treaties and to fully harmonize its regulations and implementing rules with them. Compliance with these treaties is not required under WTO rules, but they still reflect important international norms for providing copyright protection over the Internet. These treaties have been ratified by many developed and developing countries since they entered into force in 2002. In the case of China, this type of copyright protection is especially important in light of its rapidly increasing number of Internet users, many of whom have broadband access. At the July 2005 JCCT meeting, the United States obtained China's commitment to submit the legislative package necessary for China's accession to the WIPO Internet treaties to the National People's Congress by June 2006. Although China's fulfillment of this commitment has been delayed for technical reasons relating to coordination with Hong Kong and Macau, the Standing Committee of the National People's Congress issued a notice in late December 2006 indicating that China had decided to accede to the WIPO Internet treaties. Even before that decision, China had moved forward with the harmonization of some of its regulations and implementing rules in 2005 and 2006. In May 2006, for example, the State Council adopted an important Internet-related measure, the Regulations on the Protection of Copyright Over Information Networks, which went into effect in July 2006. Overall, this measure represents a welcome step, demonstrating China's determination to improve protection of the Internet-based right of communication to the public while China continues its preparations for accession to the WIPO Internet treaties. This measure is not comprehensive, however. A number of gaps remain to be filled for China to meet the challenges of Internet piracy and fully implement the WIPO Internet treaties.

With respect to software piracy, China issued new rules during the run-up to the 2006 JCCT meeting that require computers to be pre-installed with licensed operating system software and government agencies to purchase only computers satisfying this requirement. Combined with ongoing implementation of previous JCCT commitments on software piracy, it is hoped that these rules will contribute to significant further reductions in industry losses due to software piracy, which were estimated to have declined from $1.48 billion in 2004 to $1.27 billion in 2005. Achieving sustained reductions in end-user software piracy will require more enforcement by China's authorities, followed by high profile publicity of fines and other remedies imposed.

In the customs area, the United States was encouraged in 2006 by the Customs Administration's increased efforts to provide effective enforcement against counterfeit and pirated goods destined for export. Nevertheless, the United States remains concerned about the rapid growth in infringing products originating from China (discussed in the Enforcement section below). The United States also remains concerned about various aspects of the Regulations on the Customs Protection of Intellectual Property Rights, issued by the State Council in December 2003, and the Customs Administration's May 2004 implementing rules. Disposal of confiscated goods, for example, remains a problem under the implementing rules. Among other things, the implementing rules appear to mandate auction following removal of infringing features, rather than destruction of infringing goods not purchased by the right holder or used for public welfare. Allowing goods to re-enter the channels of commerce under these circumstances raises questions of consistency with provisions of the TRIPS Agreement and, in some cases, safety concerns. The United States raised these issues with China bilaterally and at the WTO in 2006, but so far China has not indicated that it will be addressing them.

The United States also remains concerned about a variety of weaknesses in China's legal framework that do not effectively deter, and may even encourage, certain types of infringing activity, such as the abusive registration of trademarks, the "squatting" of foreign company names and designs, the theft of trade secrets, the registration of other companies' trademarks as design patents and vice versa, the use of falsified or misleading license documents or company documentation to create the appearance of legitimacy in counterfeiting operations, and false indications of geographic origin of products. In 2006, the United States continued to discuss these and other problems with China and seek solutions for them.

In the pharmaceuticals sector, the United States continues to have a range of concerns. The United States has urged China to provide greater protection against unfair commercial use of undisclosed test and other data submitted by foreign pharmaceuticals companies seeking marketing approval for their products. The United States has also encouraged China to undertake a more robust system of patent linkage and to consider the adoption of a system of patent term restoration. In addition, built-in delays in China's marketing approval system for pharmaceuticals continue to create incentives for counterfeiting, as does China's inadequate regulatory oversight for the production of active pharmaceutical ingredients by domestic chemical manufacturers. In 2006, as in prior years, the United States sought to address all of these issues as part of its broader effort to work with China to improve China's regulatory regime for the pharmaceuticals sector.

Enforcement

The TRIPS Agreement requires China to ensure that enforcement procedures are available so as to permit effective action against any act of infringement of intellectual property rights covered by the TRIPS Agreement, including expeditious remedies to prevent infringement and remedies that constitute a deterrent to further infringement. Although the central government displayed strong leadership in modifying the full range of China's IPR laws and regulations in an effort to bring them into line with China's WTO commitments, effective

IPR enforcement has not been achieved, and IPR infringement remains a serious problem throughout China. IPR enforcement is hampered by a lack of coordination among Chinese government ministries and agencies, a lack of training, the allocation of resources, a lack of transparency in the enforcement process and its outcomes, and local protectionism and corruption.

Despite repeated anti-piracy campaigns in China, an increasing number of civil IPR cases in Chinese courts and other efforts, overall piracy and counterfeiting levels in China remained unacceptably high in 2006. IPR infringement continued to affect products, brands and technologies from a wide range of industries, including films, music and sound recordings, publishing, business and entertainment software, pharmaceuticals, chemicals, information technology, apparel, athletic footwear, textile fabrics and floor coverings, consumer goods, food and beverages, electrical equipment, automotive parts and industrial products, among many others.

U.S. industry in 2006 continued to estimate that levels of piracy in China across all lines of copyright business range between 85 percent and 93 percent, indicating little or no improvement over 2005. Trade in pirated optical discs continues to thrive, supplied by both licensed and unlicensed factories and by smugglers. Small retail shops continue to be the major commercial outlets for pirated movies and music (and a wide variety of counterfeit goods), and roaming vendors offering cheap pirated discs continue to be visible in major cities across China. Piracy of books and journals and end-user piracy of business software also remain key concerns. In addition, Internet piracy is increasing, as is piracy over enclosed networks such as universities.

Although China made a commitment at the July 2005 JCCT meeting to take aggressive action against movie piracy, including enhanced enforcement for titles not yet authorized for distribution, right holders have monitored China's efforts and report little meaningful improvement in piracy of pre-release titles in several major cities. However, NCA began to undertake campaigns to combat Internet piracy in 2006. In addition, with the assistance of the Ministry of Education, NCA took initial steps to address textbook piracy on university campuses in late 2006. The continuation of these efforts, along with follow-up monitoring and consistent publicity, are needed to create lasting improvements.

China's widespread counterfeiting not only harms the business interests of foreign right holders, but also includes many products that pose a direct threat to the health and safety of consumers in the United States, China and elsewhere, such as pharmaceuticals, food and beverages, batteries, automotive parts, industrial equipment and toys, among many other products. At the same time, the harm from counterfeiting is not limited to right holders and consumers. China estimated its own annual tax losses due to counterfeiting at more than $3.2 billion in 2002, and this figure could only have grown in the ensuing years.

The United States places the highest priority on addressing the IPR protection and enforcement problems in China, and since 2004 it has devoted significant additional staff and resources, both in Washington and in Beijing, to address these problems. A domestic Chinese business constituency is also increasingly active in promoting IPR protection and enforcement. In fact, Chinese right holders own the vast majority of design patents, utility models, trademarks and plant varieties in China and have become the principal filers of invention patents. In addition, the vast majority of China's IPR enforcement efforts are undertaken at the behest of Chinese right holders seeking to protect their interests. Nevertheless, it is clear that there will continue to be a need for sustained efforts from the United States and other WTO Members and their industries, along with the devotion of considerable resources and political will to IPR protection and enforcement by the Chinese government, if significant improvements are to be achieved.

As in prior years, the United States worked with central and local government officials in China in 2006 in a determined and sustained effort to improve China's IPR enforcement, with a particular emphasis on the need for dramatically increased utilization of criminal remedies. A variety of U.S. agencies held regular bilateral discussions with their Chinese counterparts and have conducted numerous technical assistance programs for central and local government officials on TRIPS Agreement rules, enforcement methods, patent and trademark practices and procedures, transparency and rule of law issues. In addition, in 2006, the United States organized another annual roundtable meeting in China designed to bring together U.S. and Chinese government and industry officials. The United States also continued to use the IPR Working Group created at the April 2004 JCCT meeting and the JCCT process itself to press China for needed changes.

The United States' efforts have also benefited from cooperation with other WTO Members in seeking improvements in China's IPR enforcement, both in China and at the WTO during meetings of the TRIPS Council. For example, the United States, Japan and Switzerland made coordinated requests under Article

63.3 of the TRIPS Agreement in October 2005 in order to obtain more information about IPR infringement levels and enforcement activities in China and provide a better basis for assessing the effectiveness of China's efforts to improve IPR enforcement since China's accession to the WTO. In addition, the United States and the EC have increased coordination and information sharing on a range of China IPR issues over the last year. China's membership in the Asia Pacific Economic Cooperation Forum (APEC) also brings increased importance to APEC's work to develop regional IPR best practices.

The United States has also continued to pursue a comprehensive initiative to combat the enormous global trade in counterfeit and pirated goods, including exports of infringing goods from China to the United States and the rest of the world. That initiative, the Strategy Targeting Organized Piracy (STOP!), was announced in October 2004 and is a U.S. Government wide effort to stop fakes at the U.S. border, to empower U.S. businesses to secure and enforce their intellectual property rights in overseas markets, to expose international counterfeiters and pirates, to keep global supply chains free of infringing goods, to dismantle criminal enterprises that steal U.S. intellectual property and to reach out to like-minded U.S. trading partners in order to build an international coalition to stop counterfeiting and piracy worldwide.

China's share of infringing goods seized at the U.S. border increased from 69 percent in Fiscal Year 2005 to 81 percent in Fiscal Year 2006, with the value of infringing goods from China totaling more than $125 million. The continuing growth in both the absolute value and China's relative share of infringing goods seized at the border is a major challenge that calls for serious actions by the Chinese government.

China is making genuine efforts to improve IPR enforcement. U.S. industry has confirmed that some of China's special campaigns, such as the continuing "Mountain Eagle" campaign against trademark infringement crimes, have in fact resulted in increased arrests and seizures of infringing materials, although the disposition of seized goods and the outcomes of criminal cases remain largely obscured by a lack of transparency. The 2006 Action Plan announced that China will launch more of these "special crackdown efforts" with respect to various IPR infringement problems. The United States has urged China to use its implementation of the 2006 Action Plan as an opportunity to tackle emerging enforcement challenges, particularly the sale of pirated and counterfeit goods on the Internet. In addition, the United States has suggested that China use this opportunity to examine the potential benefits of specialized national IPR courts and prosecutors, providing faster trademark examination procedures and ensuring that the resources available to local administrative, police and judicial authorities charged with protecting and enforcing intellectual property rights are adequate to the task.

Nevertheless, despite its many positive efforts to improve IPR enforcement, China pursues other policies that continue to impede effective enforcement. China refuses to make needed changes to its legal framework that would facilitate the utilization of criminal remedies. These changes should be an important objective for China, given the lack of deterrence clearly evident in China's current enforcement regime, which relies too heavily on administrative enforcement. But,

China continues to maintain counter-productive measures such as its high thresholds for criminal prosecution, which continue to constrain China's enforcement authorities while creating a "safe harbor" for substantial commercial-scale infringement. At the same time, China maintains market access barriers, such as import restrictions and restrictions on wholesale and retail distribution, which discourage and delay the introduction of a number of legitimate foreign products into China's market. These barriers create additional incentives for infringement of products like movies, video games and books and inevitably lead consumers to the black market, again compounding the severe problems already faced by China's enforcement authorities.

Chapter 7

SERVICES BARRIERS

Until China's entry into the WTO, China's service sectors were among the most heavily regulated and protected sectors of the national economy. Foreign service providers were largely restricted to operations under the terms of selective "experimental" licenses. However, both as a matter of policy and as a result of its WTO commitments, China decided to significantly liberalize foreign investment in its service sectors. At present, the market for services, underdeveloped due to historical attitudes and policies, has significant growth potential in both the short and long term.

China's WTO commitments are designed to provide meaningful access for U.S. service providers. In its accession agreement, China committed to the substantial opening of a broad range of service sectors through the elimination of many existing limitations on market access at all levels of government, particularly in sectors of importance to the United States, such as banking, insurance, distribution, telecommunications and professional services. These commitments are far-reaching, particularly when compared to the services commitments of many other WTO Members.

China also made certain "horizontal" commitments, which apply to all sectors listed in its Services Schedule. The two most important of these cross-cutting commitments involve acquired rights and the licensing process. Under the acquired rights commitment, China agreed that the conditions of ownership, operation and scope of activities for a foreign company, as set out in the respective contractual or shareholder agreement or in a license establishing or authorizing the operation or supply of services by an existing foreign service supplier, will not be made more restrictive than they were on the date of China's accession to the WTO. In other words, if a foreign company had pre-WTO accession rights that went beyond the commitments made by China in its Services Schedule that company could continue to operate with those rights.

In the licensing area, prior to China's WTO accession, foreign companies in many sectors did not have an unqualified right to apply for a license to operate in China. They could only apply for a license if they first received an invitation from the relevant Chinese regulatory authorities, and even then the decision-making process lacked transparency and was subject to inordinate delay and discretion. In its accession agreement, China committed to licensing procedures that were streamlined, transparent and more predictable.

At present, many challenges remain in securing the benefits of China's services commitments. While China continued to keep pace nominally with the openings required by its WTO accession agreement, it also continued to maintain or erect terms of entry in some sectors that were so high or cumbersome as to prevent or discourage foreign suppliers from gaining market access. For example, excessive and often discriminatory capital requirements continued to restrict market entry for foreign suppliers in many sectors, such as insurance, banking, motor vehicle financing, securities, asset management, telecommunications, construction and freight forwarding, among others. In addition, in sectors such as insurance, banking and legal services, branching and related restrictions have been put into effect that raise concerns. In other sectors, such as construction services, problematic measures appear to be taking away previously acquired market access rights.

Meanwhile, the Administrative Licensing Law, which took effect in July 2004, has increased transparency in the licensing process, while reducing procedural obstacles and strengthening the legal environment for domestic and foreign enterprises. As a result, the licensing process in many sectors continued to proceed in a workman-like fashion in 2006, although concerns about unfair discrimination remained, particularly in the banking and insurance sectors. In addition, in some sectors, such as direct selling and telecommunications, the licensing process was characterized by inordinate delays.

Insurance Services

In its WTO accession agreement, China agreed to phase in expanded ownership rights for foreign companies, for the most part during the first three years of China's WTO membership. Upon China's accession to the WTO, foreign life insurers were to be permitted to hold 50 percent equity share in a joint venture; within two years of accession, foreign property, casualty and other non-life insurers were to be permitted to establish as a branch, joint venture or a wholly foreign-owned subsidiary; and, within three years of accession, or by December 11, 2004, foreign insurers handling large scale commercial risks, marine, aviation and transport insurance, and reinsurance were to be permitted 51 percent foreign equity share in a joint venture (with the right to establish as a wholly foreign-owned subsidiary within two more years). China further agreed that all foreign insurers would be permitted to expand the scope of their activities to include group, health and pension lines of insurance by December 11, 2004. In addition, China agreed to eliminate geographic restrictions on all types of insurance operations by December 11, 2004.

With regard to branching, China scheduled a WTO commitment to allow non-life firms to establish as a branch in China upon accession and to permit internal branching in accordance with the lifting of China's geographic restrictions. China further agreed that foreign insurers already established in China that were seeking authorization to establish branches or sub-branches would not have to satisfy the requirements applicable to foreign insurers seeking a license to enter China's market.

Shortly after China acceded to the WTO, the China Insurance Regulatory Commission (CIRC) issued several new insurance regulations, including ones directed at the regulation of foreign insurance companies. These regulations implemented many of China's commitments, but they also created problems in three critical areas – capitalization requirements, transparency and branching. In particular, China's capitalization requirements were significantly more exacting than those of other major economies, and they limited the ability of foreign insurers to make necessary joint venture arrangements. The regulations also continued to permit considerable bureaucratic discretion and to offer limited predictability to foreign insurers seeking to operate in China's market.

In May 2004, CIRC issued implementing rules, the Detailed Rules on the Regulations for the Administration of Foreign-Invested Insurance Companies. These rules lowered capital requirements for national licenses from RMB500 million ($62.5 million) to RMB200 million ($25 million) and for branch offices from RMB50 million ($6.25 million) to RMB20 million ($2.5 million). These changes have been welcomed by some U.S. insurers, but others still consider them to be too high. The rules also streamlined licensing application procedures and shortened approval times, although some procedures remain unclear. Meanwhile, the rules did not adequately address branching rights, as many aspects of this issue remain vague. The rules also did not address another issue that U.S. and other foreign insurers had begun to complain about – in practice, it appeared that Chinese insurers were being granted new branch approvals on a concurrent basis (more than one branch approval at a time), while foreign insurers had only received approvals on a consecutive basis (one branch approval at a time). In addition, while the rules provide some guidance regarding foreign insurers wishing to apply for approval to convert from a branch to a subsidiary, CIRC has continued to have difficulty adhering to its own regulatory requirement that it act on applications within 60 days, as long delays are routine.

By December 2004, in accordance with its WTO commitments, China had lifted all of its geographic restrictions on foreign insurers. China also took steps in 2005 to permit foreign insurers to offer health and group insurance as well as pension/corporate annuities and increased the 50 percent ceiling on foreign ownership of joint venture insurance brokerages to 51 percent. In 2006, with all geographic restrictions having been removed and most business scope restrictions lifted, the operations of foreign insurers in China continued to grow. Currently, 47 foreign insurers, including a large number of U.S. insurers, operate in China. Foreign insurers had nearly a 7 percent share of the national market (according to data through 2005), and they continued to capture encouraging market shares in major municipalities such as Beijing (20 percent), Shanghai (17 percent), Shenzhen (10 percent) and Guangzhou (9 percent).

Banking Services

In its WTO accession agreement, China committed to a five-year phase-in for banking services by foreign banks. Specifically, China agreed that, immediately upon its accession, it would allow U.S. and other foreign banks to conduct foreign currency business without any market access or national treatment limitations and conduct domestic currency business with foreign-invested enterprises and foreign individuals, subject to certain geographic restrictions. The ability of U.S. and other foreign banks to conduct domestic currency business with Chinese enterprises and individuals was to be phased in. Within two years after accession, foreign banks were also to be able to conduct domestic currency business with Chinese enterprises, subject to certain geographic restrictions, which were to be lifted gradually over the following three years. Within five years after accession, foreign banks were to be able to conduct domestic currency business with Chinese individuals, and all geographic restrictions were to be lifted. Foreign banks were also to be permitted to provide financial leasing services at the same time that Chinese banks were permitted to do so.

Shortly after China's accession to the WTO, the People's Bank of China (PBOC) issued regulations governing foreign-funded banks, along with implementing rules, which became effective February 1, 2002. The PBOC also issued several other related measures. Although these measures kept pace with the WTO commitments that China made, it became clear that the PBOC had decided to exercise extreme caution in opening up the banking sector. In particular, it imposed working capital requirements and other prudential rules that far exceeded international norms, both for the foreign banks' headquarters and branches, which made it more difficult for foreign banks to establish and expand their market presence in China. Many of these requirements, moreover, did not apply equally to foreign and domestic banks. For example, a foreign bank branch licensed to conduct business in all currencies for both corporate and individual clients had to satisfy an operating capital requirement of RMB500 million ($62.5 million), while a domestic bank branch with the same business scope needed only RMB300 million ($37.5 million) in operating capital. In addition, the PBOC allowed foreign-funded banks to open only one branch every 12 months.

In early 2004, following extensive engagement by the United States and other WTO Members, the PBOC reduced working capital requirements for various categories of foreign banks. With the issuance of the Implementing Rules for the Administrative Regulations on Foreign-Invested Financial Institutions later that year, the China Banking Regulatory Commission (CBRC) also removed the restriction that had limited foreign-funded banks to opening only one new branch every 12 months. Meanwhile, China kept up with its commitments regarding the lifting of geographic restrictions on foreign banks conducting domestic currency business with foreign enterprises and individuals and Chinese enterprises.

One area still raising concerns involves the establishment of Chinese-foreign joint banks. In the Services Schedule accompanying its WTO accession agreement, China agreed that qualified foreign financial institutions would be permitted to establish Chinese-foreign joint banks immediately after China acceded, and it did not schedule any limitation on the percentage of foreign ownership in these banks. To date, however, China has limited the sale of equity stakes in existing state-owned banks to a single foreign investor to 20 percent, while the total equity share of all foreign investors is limited to 25 percent.

By September 2006, despite high capital requirements and other impediments, 191 foreign banks, including a number of U.S. banks, reportedly had branches or representative offices in China, although only major banks have been large enough to satisfy the application requirements. In addition, the business that foreign banks were most eager to pursue in China – domestic currency business – had expanded tremendously, although China's regulatory authorities continued to shield domestic banks from foreign competition in some areas, such as by limiting product innovation by foreign banks. According to the

PBOC and CBRC, the domestic currency business of U.S. and other foreign banks grew rapidly in the first two years after China's WTO accession, even though the banks' clients were then limited to foreign-invested enterprises and foreign individuals. Following the PBOC's December 2003 announcement that foreign banks would be permitted to conduct domestic currency business with Chinese enterprises subject to geographic restrictions allowed by China's WTO commitments, the growth in U.S. and other foreign banks' domestic currency business accelerated. By September 2006, the total assets of foreign banks in China reportedly had reached $105 billion, representing approximately 2 percent of total banking assets in China. In some coastal cities, the amount was higher. For example, in Shanghai, foreign banks' assets reportedly represented 12.4 percent of total banking assets in October 2005.

Notably, the five-year phase-in period for banking services by foreign banks was scheduled to end on December 11, 2006. By that time, China had committed to remove remaining geographic limitations and to allow foreign banks to conduct domestic currency business with Chinese individuals. Full implementation of these commitments should allow U.S. and other foreign banks to benefit tremendously from new business opportunities, and China should realize important benefits from having greater access to world-class banking services. In November 2006, however, the State Council issued the Regulations for the Administration of Foreign-Funded Banks. While the United States continues to work closely with

U.S. banks to assess these regulations, which are intended to implement China's December 11, 2006 commitments, these regulations have generated some immediate concerns. For example, the regulations mandate that only foreign-funded banks that have had a representative office in China for two years and that have total assets exceeding $10 billion can apply to incorporate in China. After incorporating, moreover, these banks only become eligible to offer full domestic currency services to Chinese individuals if they can demonstrate that they have operated in China for three years and have had two consecutive years of profits. The regulations also restrict the scope of activities that can be conducted by foreign banks seeking to operate in China through branches instead of through subsidiaries. In particular, the regulations restrict the domestic currency business of foreign bank branches. While foreign bank branches can continue to take deposits from, and make loans to, Chinese enterprises in domestic currency, they can only take domestic currency deposits of RMB1 million ($125,000) or more from Chinese individuals and cannot make any domestic currency loans to Chinese individuals. Foreign bank branches also cannot issue domestic currency credit cards to Chinese enterprises or Chinese individuals.

Securities Services

Pursuant to the terms of China's WTO accession agreement, foreign securities firms were to receive the right to form joint ventures for fund management upon China's accession to the WTO in December 2001, while joint ventures for securities underwriting were to be permitted within three years after accession.

The China Securities Regulatory Commission (CSRC) issued regulations on the establishment of joint venture fund management companies and securities underwriting by Chinese-foreign joint ventures shortly after China's WTO accession. China's decision to limit foreign partners to a minority stake of these joint ventures (49 percent for fund management and 33 percent for securities trading), however, continues to limit their appeal to leading foreign firms and only a handful of joint ventures have been formed. In addition, China continues to limit the security underwriting joint ventures to underwriting A-shares and to underwriting and trading government and corporate debt, B-shares and H-shares. In December 2005, CSRC instituted a moratorium on foreign investment in the securities sector, claiming the need to clean up domestic securities companies and further develop the sector. The Chinese stock market performed well in 2006, and some observers were predicting that CSRC may lift the moratorium in the second half of 2007.

Since December 2002, China has allowed Qualified Foreign Institutional Investors (QFIIs) to trade in A-shares via special accounts opened at designated custodian banks. In 2006, prior stringent criteria were loosened considerably, allowing more foreign institutions to qualify as QFIIs. However, other requirements limit the extent to which QFIIs can trade in A-shares. In addition, by the end of 2006, CSRC had distributed over $9 billion of the $10 billion overall QFII quota, but had not indicated when it will increase the quota.

Financial Information Services

In its WTO accession agreement, China committed that, for the services included in its Services Schedule, the relevant regulatory authorities would be separate from and not accountable to, any service suppliers they regulated, with two specified exceptions. One of the services included in China's Services Schedule – and not listed as an exception – is the "provision and transfer of financial information, and financial data processing and related software by suppliers of other financial services."

Nevertheless, concerns have been raised that China has still not established an independent regulator in the financial information services sector. Xinhua, the Chinese state news agency, is both a major market competitor of, and the regulator of, foreign financial information service providers in China.

In September 2006, a major problem developed when Xinhua issued the Administrative Measures on News and Information Release by Foreign News Agencies within China. These rules abolished the Measures for Administering the Release of Economic Information in China by Foreign News Agencies and Their Information Subsidiaries, which had been issued in 1996. Among other things, under one aspect of the 2006 rules, which has not yet been implemented, Xinhua would preclude foreign providers of financial information services from contracting directly with, or providing financial information services directly to, domestic Chinese clients. Instead, foreign financial information service providers would have to operate through a Xinhua-designated agent, and the one agent designated to date is a Xinhua affiliate. These new restrictions do not apply to domestic financial information service providers and, in addition, contrast with the rights previously enjoyed by foreign information service providers since the issuance of the 1996 rules, well before China's accession to the WTO in December 2001.

In response to complaints from the United States and the European Union, China's Premier publicly promised in September 2006 that the new rules would not change how foreign financial information service providers did business in China. Shortly thereafter, Xinhua told foreign financial information service providers that the new rules would not be applied to them until after an implementing measure was issued, although Xinhua subsequently began to pressure foreign financial information service providers to comply with the new restrictions.

Credit Cards

In the Services Schedule accompanying its Protocol of Accession, China committed to remove market access limitations and provide national treatment for foreign suppliers providing "payment and money transmission services, including credit, charge, and debit cards," with this commitment becoming effective with regard to the RMB business of retail clients no later than December 11, 2006. China also extended this commitment to cover the provision and transfer of financial information, financial data processing and advisory, intermediation and other financial services auxiliary to payments and money transmission services.

Under its existing rules, China restricts access to its market by foreign credit card companies. The rules only permit a bank in China to issue a credit card with a foreign logo on it if the card is co-branded with the logo of China Union Pay (CUP), an entity created by the PBOC and owned by participating Chinese banks. In addition, all RMB transactions must be processed through CUP's network, while the network of the foreign credit card company is used only to process foreign currency transactions.

In the second half of 2006, a number of troubling proposals were attributed to CUP and apparently supported by the PBOC. The common theme of these proposals was that CUP would be designated as a monopoly provider of payment and money transmission services for Chinese consumers for RMB processing and that no other providers would be able to enter this market. To date, China has taken no steps to implement its commitment to open up its market to foreign credit card companies. China reportedly is in the process of drafting regulations in this area, but no drafts have been made publicly available.

Wholesaling Services and Commission Agents' Services

In its WTO accession agreement, China committed to provide national treatment and eliminate market access restrictions for foreign enterprises seeking to provide wholesaling and commission agents' services and related services, such as repair and maintenance services, through a local presence within three years of China's accession (or by December 11, 2004), subject to limited product exceptions. In the interim, China agreed to progressively liberalize its treatment of these services pursuant to a set schedule. The phase-in of these services was supposed to start with minority foreign-owned joint ventures by December 11, 2002, followed by majority foreign-owned joint ventures by December 11, 2003.

Shortly after acceding to the WTO, China fell behind in its implementation of the required progressive liberalization, as foreign enterprises continued to face a variety of restrictions. It was not until mid-2004, following high-level U.S. engagement that China began to take steps to liberalize. At that time, MOFCOM issued regulations providing national treatment and eliminating market access restrictions on joint ventures providing wholesaling services and commission agents' services. These regulations also established a timetable for extending this liberalization to wholly foreign-owned enterprises on December 11, 2004.

While these regulations were welcome, MOFCOM was very slow to implement them, and it still has not implemented them fully. Initially, MOFCOM did not issue any guidance regarding how its approval system would operate, and the application process remained opaque. In most instances, the application process turned into a protracted negotiation, as the central and local approving authorities were still in the process of determining the appropriate procedures and documentation requirements. When approvals were issued, moreover, the central and local approving authorities imposed a variety of restrictions, such as limits on the scope of products that could be distributed and limits on the specific services that could be supplied. Registered capital requirements have also varied.

In addition, through the first six months of 2005, the Chinese authorities rarely issued approvals for existing enterprises seeking to expand their business scope to include wholesale distribution, in part because the Chinese authorities were sorting out historical tax treatment and Free Trade Zone (FTZ) issues. The Chinese authorities did issue some approvals for the establishment of new wholesale distribution enterprises, but this route did not make business sense for many enterprises already established in China.

By June 2005, the Chinese authorities had begun to make progress in resolving many of the problems that had plagued the application and approval process, including how it would handle the tax and FTZ issues that had stalled many enterprises' applications. In July 2005, MOFCOM and the General Administration of Customs (Customs Administration) issued the Circular on Issues Concerning the Trade Administration of Bonded Zones and Bonded Logistics Parks, which clarified the handling of applications from enterprises located in FTZs. At the July 2005 JCCT meeting, China also committed to improve the transparency of the application and approval process. Consistent with this commitment, in September 2005, MOFCOM issued the Application and Approval Guidelines for Foreign Investments, which clarify many aspects of the application and approval process. Some improvements subsequently took place in the application and approval process, but it was not until MOFCOM issued the Notice on Entrusting National Economic and Technological Development Zones with the Authority to Approve Foreign-Funded Distribution Firms and International Forwarding Agents in February 2006 that the problems with the application and approval process largely disappeared. With the issuance of that measure, MOFCOM devolved the right to grant distribution licenses from the central authorities to provincial-level authorities, making the application and approval process more efficient and less time-consuming, although some technical challenges remain with regard to, for example, manufacturing enterprises seeking to expand the scope of their business to include distribution activities.

These developments have enabled U.S. companies to improve the efficiency of their China supply chain management, and as a result many of them are restructuring their legal entities to integrate their China operations into their global business more fully and efficiently. At the same time, U.S. companies in some industries continue to have concerns with regard to product and services restrictions that China has yet to remove.

U.S. industry remains seriously concerned about continuing restrictions on the rights of foreign enterprises to engage in wholesale (and retail) distribution of books, newspapers, periodicals, electronic publications and audio and video products. Some measures, such as the April 2004 distribution services regulations, purport to allow foreign enterprises to engage in wholesale (and retail) distribution of these products. However, a host of other measures appear to impose market access or national treatment limitations, such as the State Council's April 2005 Several Opinions on Canvassing Foreign Investment into the Cultural Sector; NDRC's November 2004 Catalogue for the Guidance of Foreign Investment Industries; the Provisions on the Administration of the Publication Market, issued by the General Administration of Press and Publication (GAPP) in June 2004; the Rule on Management of Foreign-Invested Book, Magazine and Newspaper Distribution Enterprises, issued by GAPP and MOFTEC in March 2003; and the Administrative Regulations on Electronic Publications, issued by GAPP in December 1997. Under these measures, for some of the products at issue, distribution is limited to Chinese state-owned enterprises. For others, only Chinese-foreign joint ventures with minority foreign ownership are permitted to engage in distribution or foreign enterprises face restrictive requirements not imposed on domestic enterprises.

China began to implement several measures governing the distribution of automobiles by foreign enterprises in 2005, including the Implementing Rules for the Administration of Brand-Specific Automobile Dealerships, jointly issued by MOFCOM, the NDRC and the State Administration for Industry and Commerce (SAIC) in February 2005. The NDRC followed up with the Rules for Auto External Marks in November 2005, and MOFCOM issued the Implementing Rules for the Evaluation of Eligibility of Auto General Distributors and Brand-specific Dealers in January 2006. While U.S. industry has generally welcomed these measures, they do contain some restrictions on foreign enterprises that may not be applied to domestic enterprises.

China delayed the implementation of its wholesale distribution services commitments with regard to pharmaceuticals, despite the fact that the exception for pharmaceuticals contained in China's accession agreement expired as of December 11, 2004. Although the April 2004 distribution services regulations indicated that separate regulations would be issued for the pharmaceuticals sector, China did not issue any further regulations and continued to require foreign pharmaceutical companies to sell their finished products through Chinese wholesalers (after hiring Chinese importers to bring their finished products into the country) through the remainder of 2004 and the first half of 2005. In the second half of 2005, China began allowing the acceptance of applications from foreign pharmaceutical companies for wholesale distribution licenses under the April 2004 distribution services regulations and the State Food and Drug Administration's Rules on the Management of Drug Business Licenses. Since then, U.S. and other foreign pharmaceutical companies have been able to obtain wholesale distribution licenses. However, it appears that some provincial-level authorities have not yet begun issuing these licenses because of uncertainty generated by the provision in the April 2004 distribution services regulations indicating that MOFCOM would issue separate regulations covering pharmaceuticals. At the same time, despite overall progress in this area, many other restrictions affecting the pharmaceuticals sector make it difficult for foreign pharmaceutical companies to realize the full benefits of China's wholesale distribution commitments. The United States continues to engage the Chinese regulatory authorities in these areas as part of an effort to promote comprehensive reform of China's healthcare system and to reduce unnecessary trade barriers.

U.S. industry remains concerned about the uncertainty created by the provision in the April 2004 distribution services regulations that allows the local approving authorities to withhold wholesale (and retail) distribution license approvals when, as is the case in most cities, urban commercial network plans have not yet been formulated. This provision could operate as a *de facto* restriction on the operations of foreign wholesalers (and retailers).

In early December 2006, China issued the Measures for the Administration of the Market for Crude Oil and the Measures for the Administration of the Market for Refined Oil Products. These measures are intended to implement China's significant market-opening WTO commitments, scheduled for December 11, 2006, to permit foreign enterprises to engage in wholesale distribution of crude oil and processed oil (e.g., gasoline), in China. China's full implementation of these commitments would allow U.S. industry to begin to take advantage of China's earlier, partial opening of the retail distribution sector to foreign enterprises. However, these regulations impose high thresholds and other potential impediments on foreign enterprises seeking to enter the wholesale distribution sector, such as requirements relating to levels of storage capacity, pipelines, rail lines, docks and supply contracts. These requirements appear designed to maintain the monopolies enjoyed by state-owned China National Petroleum Corporation and China Petrochemical Corporation.

Retailing Services

In 1999, the Chinese government broadened the scope for foreign investment in the retail sector. New regulations encouraged the entry of large international retailers (such as hypermarkets and warehouse-style stores) into China. China's subsequent WTO commitments were designed to further expand the ability of foreign retailers to enter the market through a much wider range of modalities. China committed to allow 100 percent foreign ownership of smaller retail operations, some large retail operations, gas stations and even car dealerships within three years to five years of China's December 2001 WTO accession, although certain types of large retail operations could still face ownership limitations.

As in the area of wholesaling and commission agents' services, China fell behind in its implementation of the required progressive liberalization of retailing services shortly after acceding to the WTO, as foreign enterprises continued to face a variety of restrictions. China only began to take steps to liberalize in mid-2004, when MOFCOM issued regulations providing national treatment and eliminating market access restrictions on joint ventures supplying retailing services. These regulations also established a timetable for extending this liberalization to wholly foreign-owned enterprises on December 11, 2004.

Many of the same problems that plagued the application and approval process for wholesaling and commission agents' services also arose in the area of retailing services. The changes that took place in the application and approval process in 2005 helped to improve the situation, but it was MOFCOM's issuance of the Notice on Entrusting National Economic and Technological Development Zones with the Authority to Approve Foreign-Funded Distribution Firms and International Forwarding Agents in February 2006 that made the problems with the application and approval process largely disappear.

U.S. industry continues to have concerns with regard to the provision in the April 2004 distribution services regulations allowing the approving authorities to withhold retail distribution license approvals when, as is the case in many cities, urban commercial network plans have not yet been formulated. It appears that China may be applying this provision in a discriminatory manner. In April 2006, MOFCOM issued a notice explaining that foreign-invested enterprises would not be granted approvals for projects in cities that had not yet finalized their urban commercial network plans, while it appears that domestic enterprises continue to receive approvals for their projects.

Meanwhile, it appears that China may not be fully implementing its commitment to allow foreign enterprises to sell gasoline at the retail level.

Although China's retail services commitments initially did not apply to processed oil, as it was one of the excepted goods under China's Services Schedule, that exception expired on December 11, 2004, and by that time China committed to permit wholly foreign-owned enterprises to operate gas stations. However, according to some recent reports, China is now claiming that gas stations fall under the chain store provision in its Services Schedule, which applies to "those chain stores which sell products of different types and brands from multiple suppliers with more than 30 outlets" and permits only joint ventures with minority foreign ownership.

Franchising Services

As part of its services commitments, China committed to permit the cross-border supply of franchising services immediately upon its accession to the WTO. It also committed to permit foreign enterprises to provide franchising services in China, without any market access or national treatment limitations, by December 11, 2004. In December 2004, MOFCOM issued new rules governing the supply of franchising services in China, the Measures for the Administration of Commercial Franchises, which became effective in February 2005. These rules raised a number of concerns. Of particular concern is a requirement that a franchiser own and operate at least two units in China for one year before being eligible to offer franchises in China. The business models of many U.S. franchising companies, including some large hotel chains, are adversely affected by this requirement because they do not own and operate units, instead relying exclusively on franchisees to distribute goods and services. The rules also impose high capital requirements and require broad and vague information disclosure by franchisers, with uncertain liability if these disclosure requirements are not met. Following U.S. Government and U.S. industry requests that China address these issues by revising the December 2005 franchising rules, China reported in November 2006 that revised franchising rules had been submitted to the State Council for review and would be issued in due course.

Sales Away from a Fixed Location

In 1998, China banned all direct selling activities (or sales away from a fixed location) after some foreign and domestic firms used direct selling techniques to operate fraudulent pyramid schemes and other less-than-legitimate operations disguised as direct selling to bilk participants. No U.S. firms were implicated in these schemes. Meanwhile, some large U.S. and other foreign direct selling firms were allowed to continue operating in China after altering their business models. In its WTO accession agreement, China committed to the resumption of direct selling activities by December 2004.

In August and September 2005, nine months overdue, the Chinese authorities issued the measures designed to implement China's direct selling commitments – the Measures for the Administration of Direct Selling and the Regulations on the Administration of Anti-Pyramid Sales Scams. These measures became effective on December 1, 2005, and contained several problematic provisions. For example, one provision outlaws practices allowed in every country in which the U.S. industry operates – reportedly 170 countries in all – by refusing to allow direct selling enterprises to pay compensation based on team sales, where upstream personnel are compensated based on downstream sales. In addition, there is a cap limiting the amount of compensation based on sales revenue to 30 percent, which inhibits direct selling companies from employing compensation as a tool to motivate their sales representatives. Other problematic provisions in the 2005 measures include onerous and vague requirements to establish fixed location "service centers" in each urban district where direct sellers operate; a three-year experience requirement that only applies to foreign enterprises, not domestic ones; restrictions on the cross-border supply of direct selling services; limited product categories permitted for direct sales; and high capital requirements that may limit smaller direct sellers' access to the market. The measures also impose burdensome education and certification requirements for salespersons and trainers, forbidding foreigners from working in either capacity.

In September 2006, China issued implementing rules governing the establishment of direct selling service centers. These rules, while clarifying some aspects of the earlier measures, also include vague provisions that could lead to undue local requirements being placed on service centers. The rules should streamline service center requirements at the national level.

Under the 2005 measures, a direct selling company must receive approvals from both MOFCOM and SAIC before beginning operations. MOFCOM issued its first direct selling license approval under the 2005 measures in February 2006 and had approved 15 licenses to Chinese and foreign companies by the end of 2006. Despite this progress, the MOFCOM licensing process has been characterized by a lack of transparency and significant delays. The 2005 measures establish a 90-day license approval process, but most of the MOFCOM approvals took between 4 months and 11 months. In addition, according to U.S. industry, more than 20 companies that applied for direct selling licenses in early 2006 are still awaiting approval, with little clarity on timing or process. The scope of licenses approved by MOFCOM has also been limited, with only three companies approved to conduct direct selling in more than one province in China. Meanwhile, few companies have received the SAIC approval necessary to begin operations.

Express Delivery Services

Beginning in December 2001, the State Postal Bureau (together with MOFTEC and MII) issued restrictive measures that could have jeopardized market access that foreign express delivery firms (which were then required to operate as joint ventures with Chinese partners) enjoyed prior to China's accession. These measures threatened to curtail the scope of operations of foreign express delivery firms licensed prior to China's accession to the WTO, despite China's horizontal commitment on acquired rights. Specifically, a measure issued in December 2001 required firms wishing to deliver letters to apply for entrustment with China Post. A second measure, issued in February 2002, extended China Post's monopoly on letters by creating weight and rate restrictions on letter deliveries by private firms. Following high-level U.S. interventions, in September 2002, a third measure eliminated the weight and rate restrictions on letter deliveries and streamlined the entrustment application procedure. Two major

U.S. express delivery firms subsequently applied for and obtained entrustment certificates from China Post.

In July 2003, however, China circulated draft amendments to its Postal Law that generated two immediate concerns among U.S. companies. First, the draft amendments purported to give China Post a monopoly over the delivery of letters under 500 grams, which would have constituted a new restriction on the scope of activities of existing foreign-invested express delivery companies, raising concerns in light of China's horizontal acquired rights commitment. Second, the draft amendments did not address the need for an independent regulator.

In September, October and November 2003, China circulated new sets of draft Postal Law amendments. While each set of draft amendments included a different definition of the China Post monopoly, the most recent draft amendments continued to provide China Post with a monopoly on letters weighing less than 500 grams. They also included other problematic provisions. For example, they appeared to create a new, more burdensome licensing process, and they seemed to require express couriers to pay a percentage of their revenue from the delivery of letters into a universal service fund.

In April 2004, following high-level U.S. engagement urging China not to cut back on the scope of activities that foreign-invested express delivery companies had been licensed to provide prior to China's WTO accession, Vice Premier Wu Yi committed that old problems, like the weight restriction, would not resurface as new problems. In July 2004, however, the State Council circulated another set of draft amendments to the postal services law. Despite Vice Premier Wu's commitment, these draft amendments continued to include a weight restriction, now reduced from 500 grams to 350 grams and did little to address other U.S. concerns.

In April 2006, as more reports began to surface of problematic provisions in subsequent drafts of the Postal Law, Vice Premier Wu Yi reiterated China's commitment that the regulatory environment for express delivery services by foreign companies would not be negatively impacted by the issuance of new rules, including the Postal Law. Later in 2006, however, China began to circulate an "eighth" draft of the Postal Law among Chinese stakeholders, and this draft continued to generate serious concerns. Although this draft has not been officially released, it reportedly would impose a minimum weight restriction on addressed letters weighing less than 150 grams, exclude foreign service providers from the domestic express delivery market and impose a tax to fund universal mail service in China. When the United States raised concerns about this "eighth" draft both bilaterally and at the WTO in October 2006 and November 2006, Chinese government officials responded that the draft is undergoing major revisions.

Meanwhile, in August 2006, the State Council began implementing its July 2005 plan to separate China's postal operations from the administrative function of regulating China's postal system, with the State Postal Administration (SPA) to serve as the regulator and a new state-owned enterprise – the China Post Group Corporation – to be set up to conduct postal business. Although the July 2005 plan has still not been released to the public, SPA announced the establishment of 31 provincial-level Postal Management Bureaus to assist in the regulatory effort in September 2006. The China Post Group Corporation was established in January 2007.

Construction, Engineering, Architectural and Contracting Services

Prior to China's WTO accession, U.S. construction, engineering and architectural firms and U.S. contractors enjoyed a relatively cooperative and open relationship with the Chinese government. These firms operated in the Chinese market through joint venture arrangements and were less affected by regulatory problems than other service sectors. Nevertheless, they also faced restrictions. It was difficult for foreign firms to obtain licenses to perform services except on a project-by-project basis. Foreign firms also faced severe partnering and bidding restrictions.

In September 2002, the Ministry of Construction and MOFTEC jointly issued Decrees 113 and 114, which opened up construction and related construction design services to joint ventures with majority foreign ownership and, two years ahead of schedule, wholly foreign-owned enterprises. At the same time, however, these decrees created concerns for U.S. and other foreign firms by imposing new and more restrictive conditions than existed prior to China's WTO accession, when they were permitted to work in China on a project-by-project basis pursuant to Ministry of Construction rules. In particular, these decrees for the first time required foreign firms to obtain qualification certificates, effective October 2003. In addition, these decrees for the first time required foreign-invested firms supplying construction services to incorporate in China, and they imposed high minimum registered capital requirements and foreign personnel residency requirements that are difficult for many foreign firms to satisfy. In consultation with

U.S. industry, the United States, in a high-level intervention, pressed its concerns about Decrees 113 and 114 and sought a delay before the decrees' problematic requirements would become effective. In September 2003, the Ministry of Construction agreed to extend the implementation date from October 2003 until April 2004 so the concerns of foreign firms could be analyzed further.

In April 2004, Decree 113 went into effect. However, in September 2004, the Ministry of Construction and MOFCOM issued Circular 159, which permitted foreign providers of construction services and related construction engineering design services to continue operating on a project by-project basis until July 2005, effectively extending the effective date of the incorporation-related requirements.

Decree 114 implementing rules were released and became effective in January 2007. These rules allow the Chinese authorities to begin accepting applications from foreign-invested enterprises, including wholly foreign-owned enterprises, seeking to provide engineering, integrated engineering and architectural services. The rules also make several positive regulatory changes, including the temporary lifting of foreign personnel staffing and residency requirements for foreign-invested design companies.

Meanwhile, in November 2004, the Ministry of Construction issued the Provisional Measures for Construction Project Management (known as Decree

200), which became effective in December 2004. Among other things, Decree 200 appears to preclude the same company from providing construction services and related construction engineering design services if it also provides project management services on the same project. This aspect of the decree raises concerns because U.S. companies often provide all of these services in combination when working on a project in a foreign market. No implementing regulations for Decree 200 have been issued.

Transportation and Logistics Services

The transportation and logistics sector has in the past faced severe regulatory restrictions, high costs, dominance by government-invested agents and limitations on permitted activities. The multiple government bodies responsible for this sector include the Ministry of Communications, the Ministry of Railways, MOFCOM, NDRC and the Civil Aviation Administration of China. Overlapping jurisdictions, multiple sets of approval requirements and opaque regulations hinder market access. In some areas, domestic firms have also used government connections and investments to monopolize the sector.

Nevertheless, like China's own reform policies, China's WTO commitments support a broad opening of the transportation and logistics sector to foreign service providers, to be phased in over time. Foreign firms should be able to invest freely in warehousing, road freight transport, rail freight transport and freight forwarding companies within three years to six years after WTO accession, depending on the sector.

In July 2002, MOFCOM's predecessor, MOFTEC, issued a Notice on Establishing Foreign-Invested Logistics Companies in Trial Regions. This notice allows foreign-invested logistics companies (with up to 50 percent foreign ownership and registered capital of $5 million) to establish in several designated cities. U.S. firms have expressed concern about the high capital requirement and the 50 percent cap on foreign ownership, which may conflict with China's WTO commitments for certain types of logistics services.

In November 2002, China issued regulations allowing majority foreign ownership of road transportation firms, as it was required to do within one year of its WTO accession. China was also obligated to issue regulations allowing majority foreign-owned joint ventures to enter the fields of packaging services, storage and warehousing, and freight forwarding one year after its accession; it issued timely regulations allowing 75 percent foreign-owned joint ventures in these fields.

China took a significant step in July 2004 to increase market access for U.S. passenger and cargo carriers by signing a landmark amendment to the aviation agreement with the United States. The amended agreement will more than double the number of U.S. airlines operating in China and will increase by five times the number of flights providing passenger and cargo services between the two countries over the next six years. The agreement also allows each country's carriers to serve any city in the other country, provides for unlimited code-sharing between them, expands opportunities for charter operators, and eliminates government regulation of pricing as of 2008. U.S. passenger and cargo carriers have since obtained additional routes and increased flight frequencies, as envisioned by the agreement. Meanwhile, an important commitment enshrined in the July 2004 agreement calls for the commencement of negotiations toward further liberalization through a bilateral Open Skies Agreement. The first round of these negotiations took place in April 2006. However, China subsequently postponed the second round of negotiations. In December 2006, at the inaugural meeting of U.S.-China Strategic Economic Dialogue (SED) in Beijing, the United States and China agreed to resume work toward liberalization of the aviation relationship with the mutually agreed goal of making meaningful progress in time for the second SED meeting, tentatively scheduled for May 2007. U.S. and Chinese civil aviation delegations resumed negotiations in January 2007.

In 2003, China took steps to liberalize the maritime services sector despite having made limited WTO commitments. The United States and China signed a far-reaching, five-year bilateral maritime agreement, which gave U.S.-registered companies the legal flexibility to perform an extensive range of additional shipping and logistics activities in China. U.S. shipping and container transport services companies, along with their subsidiaries, affiliates and joint ventures are also able to establish branch offices in China without geographic limitation.

In April 2005, AQSIQ issued the Criteria for the Classification and Assessment of Logistics Firms. Under this measure, AQSIQ uses a firm's business and financial situation, equipment, operating infrastructure, management, services provided and human resource information as of the time of its business license application in order to classify the firm into one of three broad categories: transport, warehouse or multi-service, for regulatory purposes. Some firms have criticized this measure as creating "hastily formulated standards" that inappropriately restrict the business scope of logistics firms and have also complained about unnecessary and burdensome requirements. In addition, freight forwarding firms are concerned about not being included in one of the three logistics business categories, particularly because it may prevent their participation in relevant standards-setting activities.

Telecommunications

In its WTO accession agreement, China made important commitments in the area of telecommunications services. It agreed to permit foreign suppliers to provide a broad range of services through joint ventures with Chinese companies, including domestic and international wired services, mobile voice and data services, value-added services, such as electronic mail, voice mail and on-line information and database retrieval, and paging services. The foreign stake permitted in the joint ventures is to increase over time, reaching a maximum of 49 percent for most types of services. In addition, China agreed to eliminate all geographical restrictions within two to six years after its WTO accession, depending on the particular service sector.

Importantly, when it acceded to the WTO, China also accepted key regulatory principles from the WTO Reference Paper. As a result, China became obligated to separate the regulatory and operating functions of MII (which had been both the telecommunications regulatory agency in China and the operator of China Telecom) upon its accession and to implement its regulations in an impartial manner. Since China's accession, MII has spun-off China Telecom, which now competes in the market with other telecommunications operators. While the formal separation of regulator and operator has occurred, evidence of continued MII influence over operational decisions of the telecommunications operators (e.g., relating to personnel, corporate organization and standards) suggests that regulatory independence may be far from complete. The current regulator, MII, is not structured as an independent entity as it still bears the responsibility to help develop China's information technology and telecommunications manufacturing industries.

China is also obligated to adopt pro-competitive regulatory principles, such as transparent licensing, cost-based pricing and the right of interconnection, which are necessary for foreign-invested joint ventures to compete against established operators. China appears laggard in implementing these commitments, however. For example, there is no sign that "major suppliers" in China have made their interconnection arrangements public. With practically no foreign participation in the market, it has been difficult to assess compliance with such commitments. This very lack of foreign participation, however, is indicative of a licensing regime that has not been conducive to foreign investment, in part due to a lack of transparency.

China's Regulations on Foreign-Invested Telecommunications Enterprises went into effect in January 2002. These regulations define registered-capital requirements, equity caps, requirements for Chinese and foreign partners, and licensing procedures. The regulations stipulate that foreign-invested telecommunications enterprises can undertake either basic or value-added telecommunications services. Foreign ownership may not exceed 49 percent in the case of basic telecommunications services (excluding wireless paging) and 50 percent in the case of value-added services (including wireless paging, which is otherwise categorized as a basic service). While China committed to giving foreign applicants freedom to choose potential joint venture partners, it appears that MII is interpreting requirements regarding technical qualifications to effectively exclude all but incumbent operators, foreclosing additional competition in the market. For foreign operators interested in offering international services, requirements to use a gateway operated by a state-owned operator appear excessive and unjustified. The capitalization requirement established for new entrants, which exceeds $240 million, is another major impediment to market access. There appears to be no justification for such a requirement, particularly for companies interested in leasing, rather than building facilities, while specific licensing terms for resale-based operators do not appear to exist. Meanwhile, MII continues to process applications very slowly for the few foreign-invested telecommunications enterprises that have attempted to satisfy MII's licensing requirements. The results have been predictable: no new joint ventures appear to have been formed in the basic telecommunications sector since China introduced the January 2002 regulations.

At times, MII has also changed applicable rules without notice and without transparency. For example, in February 2003, MII announced a reclassification of certain basic and value-added telecommunications services effective in April 2003. No public comment period was provided. This move limited the ability of U.S. firms to access China's telecommunications market because basic services are on a slower liberalization schedule and are subject to lower foreign equity limits and higher capitalization requirements.

Little progress has been made in opening the market for value-added services, such as Internet service and content providers. MII announced moves toward convergence in voice, video and data services in 2000, but China considers information content sensitive, so foreign companies face significant barriers in the Internet services sector. Although more foreign companies are registering ".com.cn" websites in China, these sites are still often blocked, which hinders companies' abilities to maintain a stable Internet presence. The requirement that Internet service providers (ISPs) must provide user login information and transaction records to authorities upon request, without clear guidelines as to the circumstances and situations that warrant such actions, raises concerns about consumer privacy and prevention of data misuse. Meanwhile, even though China has now completed its fifth year of WTO membership, the United States is aware of only one application for a license to provide value-added services that has completed the MII licensing process. That license was awarded to a Chinese-Korean joint venture in 2005.

Foreign equity investment limitations for ISPs and Internet content providers (ICPs) mirror the timetable for value-added services in China's WTO accession agreement (30 percent upon accession, 49 percent within one year after accession and 50 percent within two years after accession). However, ICPs must still win the approval of MII and/or local telecommunications administrations depending on the geographic coverage of their services before they can receive foreign capital, cooperate with foreign businesses, or attempt domestic or overseas stock listings. Their services, including even simple commercial websites, are also subject to excessive capitalization requirements that bear little relation to any legitimate licensing goals.

In 2004, a draft of the long-awaited Telecommunications Law began to circulate among Chinese ministries and agencies. If China takes the initiative, this law could be a vehicle for addressing existing market access barriers and other problematic aspects of China's current telecommunications regime. The current status and content of this legislation is unclear, despite repeated U.S. efforts to obtain this information.

Meanwhile, even though China committed in its WTO accession agreement that further liberalization of this sector would be discussed in the current round of WTO negotiations, China has yet to make an improved services offer. With the modest telecommunications commitments made by China in its WTO accession agreement having so far failed to facilitate effective market entry for foreign firms, further liberalization, bound through the current round of WTO negotiations, appears critical to improving market access prospects for this sector.

At the April 2006 JCCT meeting, China committed to make appropriate adjustments to its registered capital requirements for telecommunications service providers. However, to date, Chinese regulators have taken no steps to adjust capitalization levels, nor have they provided any information on the timing, scope or level of any planned adjustments. China's continued imposition of excessive capital requirements, taken together with MII's reclassification of value-added services as basic services and MII's slow license application process, has kept in place formidable barriers to market entry for foreign enterprises.

On-Line Services

China operates the world's most comprehensive and technologically advanced Internet filtering regime. Chinese authorities routinely filter Internet traffic entering China, focusing primarily on the content they deem objectionable on political, social or religious grounds. In 2002, China lifted filters on most major western news sites. Nevertheless, since then, foreign news websites have periodically been blocked, as happened, for example, for several weeks during the 16th National Congress of the Communist Party of China in 2003. More generally, according to a Harvard University study published in 2002, China had still blocked 19,032 sites on multiple occasions. This study was updated in 2005, and identified routinely blocked sites that relate to Taiwan, the Falun Gong spiritual movement, Tibet, the Tiananmen Square incident and Chinese opposition political parties. The updated study also identified routinely blocked sites that relate to various political topics including "boycott," "human rights," "pro-democracy" and "opposition."

Changes to Internet filtering can occur without warning or public explanation. For example, the popular Internet search engine Google was blocked completely in China for a few weeks starting in late August 2002. When Google became available again in September 2002, its "cached pages" feature remained blocked; that feature had previously allowed users in China to access "snapshots" of some web pages that were otherwise blocked in China. While all of these practices remain prevalent, the updated study found that China's filtering regime had become more targeted and fine-tuned than in 2002. For example, sites relating to specific topics such as Falun Gong and the Tiananmen Square incident were less accessible in 2005 while sites relating vaguely to topics such as revolution and Taiwan were more accessible. Few, if any, websites related strictly to economic and business matters, however, are blocked.

China's Internet regulation regime is exceedingly complex. Internet content restrictions for ICPs, electronic commerce sites and application service providers located in China are governed by a number of measures, not all of which are public. Since 2000, these measures have increased greatly, and it is reported that at least 12 government entities have authority over Internet access and content. Some of these measures restrict who may report news and place limits on what exactly may constitute news. The most important of these measures was issued in September 2000 and updated in September 2005. In addition to interfering with news reporting in the traditional sense, this measure may provide a basis for Chinese authorities to interfere with the normal business reporting operations of non-news organizations, such as multinational corporations, if they use the

Internet to keep clients, members, their headquarters and other interested parties informed about events in China.

In March 2002, the Internet Society of China established a "Public Pledge on Self-Discipline for the China Internet Industry." This group is nominally private but is affiliated with China's Ministry of Information Industry and currently has more than 200 members. Signatories commit to "refrain from producing, posting or disseminating pernicious information that may jeopardize state security and disrupt social stability, contravene laws and regulations and spread superstition and obscenity." Reportedly, 130 major Internet portals have since signed the pledge.

Audio-Visual Services

Shortly after acceding to the WTO in December 2001, China issued the Regulations on the Administration of Audio-Visual Products and the Regulations on the Management of Film, both of which went into effect on February 1, 2002. These regulations were designed to bring more order and transparency to the audio-visual and film industries, with the objective of moving toward greater commercial efficiency in accordance with domestic reform efforts and China's WTO commitments.

Despite these positive moves and various subsequently issued regulations that provided incrementally more market access, China's desire to protect the revenues earned by the state-owned movie and print media importers and distributors, and China's concerns about politically sensitive materials, result in continued restrictions on foreign providers of audio-visual services. For example, importation and distribution of sound recordings, videos, films, books and journals remain highly restricted. Inconsistent and subjective application of censorship regulations further impedes market growth for foreign providers.

In July 2004, the State Administration for Radio, Film and TV (SARFT) issued the Rules for the Administration of China-Foreign Cooperation in Filmmaking. These rules cover filmmaking and provide for joint Chinese-foreign filmmaking cooperatives, with licenses required for both the cooperative and the Chinese partner. In October 2004, SARFT and MOFCOM issued the Provisional Rules on the Access Requirements for Film. These rules cover film production, distribution, screening and imports by domestic firms, and film production and screenings involving foreign firms. All firms engaged in these businesses are subject to SARFT licensing. Foreign firms are allowed to form joint ventures and cooperative firms engaged in film production, technology and equipment. Joint ventures or cooperative firms must have at least RMB5 million ($625,000) of registered capital, and foreign capital cannot make up more than 49 percent of the total share.

The Chinese government limits the number of foreign films allowed to enter China each year on a revenue-sharing basis. China currently allows in 20 foreign films per year (up from ten foreign films per year through much of the 1990s) on a revenue-sharing basis pursuant to a commitment that it made upon acceding to the WTO. However, China treats its WTO commitment as a ceiling, rather than a floor, which artificially increases demand for pirated products. Furthermore, lengthy censorship reviews by Chinese authorities at times can delay the arrival of legitimately imported foreign films on Chinese movie screens. When the films do make it through the censorship process, they have sometimes been subject to blackout viewing periods during national holidays and other times. China's large black market for foreign DVDs and other home entertainment video products continues to grow because these market access restrictions create a demand for pirated goods in the absence of legitimately licensed home entertainment. When legitimate products are blocked from the market by Chinese legal restrictions, demand is satisfied almost entirely by pirates. Rampant piracy also diminishes the incentive for foreign investment in movie theaters (which is currently limited to a minority stake). Some progress was achieved in 2004, when MOFCOM approved a U.S.-invested film distribution joint venture and took steps to shorten the time required to bring films to market.

In October 2004, SARFT and MOFCOM issued the Provisional Rules on the Administration of China-Foreign Joint Venture and Cooperative TV Program Production Firms. These rules establish a minimum registered capital requirement of RMB2 million ($250,000) for joint ventures and cooperative firms and mandate a share of no less than 51 percent for domestic partners. In February 2005, SARFT issued a circular placing further restrictions on foreign partners and requiring two-thirds of the programs of a joint venture or cooperative firm to have Chinese themes.

China is reportedly in the process of formulating a policy to support its weak cartoon industry. According to several reports, in June 2005, SARFT began circulating a draft measure providing that only domestically-produced cartoons could be broadcast during prime-time viewing hours and that advertisements shown during this period should be used to finance the production of domestic cartoons. The draft measure also reportedly forbids the introduction of foreign cartoons under the disguise of domestic cartoons as well as cartoons that are jointly made with foreigners. SARFT issued the final version of this measure in August 2006, and it became effective in September 2006.

Finally, in August 2005, the State Council issued a directive stating that non-public capital cannot be used to establish or operate a news agency, newspaper, publishing house, radio station or TV station. The directive also stated that radio and television signal broadcasting and relay station, satellite and backbone networks are closed to non-public capital.

Tourism and Travel Services

Since its accession to the WTO in December 2001, China has relaxed some of its restrictions on foreign operators to improve the competitiveness of its tourism and travel industries. China has also taken steps to implement its WTO commitments.

Immediately following its WTO accession, the State Council issued new travel agency regulations, the Regulations on the Administration of Travel Agencies. These regulations were designed to better enable large foreign travel and tourism service providers to participate as minority partners in operating full-service joint venture travel agencies handling foreign inbound tourism.

The China National Tourism Administration (CNTA) and MOFCOM subsequently issued the Provisional Measures for the Establishment of Foreign-Controlled and Wholly Foreign-Funded Travel Agencies, effective July 2003, which for the first time expressly allowed both foreign-controlled joint ventures and wholly foreign-owned enterprises in its travel industry. Under this measure, these travel agencies were allowed to engage in foreign inbound tourism through the establishment of offices in five major foreign tourist destinations in China (Beijing, Shanghai, Guangzhou, Shenzhen and Xian). Furthermore, the measures stipulated that foreign-controlled travel agencies must have an annual worldwide turnover in excess of $40 million, and wholly foreign-funded travel agencies must have an annual worldwide turnover in excess of $500 million. Both types of travel agencies were also subject to a local registered capital requirement of RMB4 million (approximately $500,000).

In February 2005, CNTA and MOFCOM issued a measure lowering the minimum registered capital requirement for foreign-controlled and wholly foreign-owned travel agencies from RMB4 million (approximately $500,000) to RMB2.5 million (approximately $312,500), which had been required as of December 2004 by its WTO accession agreement. It also lifted all remaining geographical restrictions on the establishment of foreign-controlled and wholly foreign-owned travel agencies, nearly three years in advance of the schedule set forth in its WTO accession agreement.

Recently, it was reported that CNTA would further ease its restrictions on foreign travel agencies operating in China beginning in July 2007. Among other proposed measures, CNTA will reportedly remove controls on the subsidiaries of foreign travel agencies and lower the capital requirements for foreign travel agencies to the same level as domestic travel agencies.

Foreign entry into China's tourism and travel industry continues to grow. In November 2003, Germany's Touristic Union International (TUI) signed a letter of intent with the China Tourism Agency to form the first foreign-controlled joint venture travel agency since China's WTO accession. Japan Airlines subsequently established the first wholly foreign-owned travel agency. By the end of 2006, China had approved the operations of 25 foreign-controlled joint venture travel agencies and wholly foreign-owned travel agencies.

The growth in China's travel and tourism industry is strong. In 2006, China hosted 22 million foreign tourists, representing an increase of 8.5 percent over the previous year. China also generated $33.5 billion in tourism revenues, making it the sixth-largest market globally. The World Tourism Council (WTC) estimates that, in 2006, growth in China's tourism and travel industry ranked second globally. The WTC also predicts sustained long-term growth in demand for China's tourism and travel industry at 8.7 percent per year (in real terms) between 2007 and 2016.

While notable improvements have been made by China, foreign firms continue to be restricted from competing under the same conditions as Chinese firms. For example, with regard to the outbound tourist market, wholly foreign-owned enterprises and Chinese-foreign joint ventures continue to be restricted in selling outbound airline tickets. In addition, China requires all travel agents, airlines and other booking entities to use or connect into China's nationally owned and operated computer reservation system when booking airline tickets. Meanwhile, holders of official Chinese passports are required to use China's state-owned airlines or their code-share partners. Nearly 23,000 holders of official Chinese passports were issued U.S. visas (in 2004), and most of them were employees of state-owned enterprises, who would not be considered government employees in most countries. This represents a significant loss of business for U.S. airlines.

At the same time, the United States has increased its visa options to Chinese nationals visiting the United States. Beginning in January 2005, eligible Chinese nationals wishing to visit the United States temporarily for business (B-1) or tourism (B-2) could be issued visas that were valid for 12 months and multiple entries. The previous maximum length of visas issued for these purposes was six months and multiple entries. Additionally, since November 2006, U.S.-bound tour parties from seven Chinese travel agencies have been allowed to apply for group visas as opposed to previously required business visas.

Education and Training Services

China faces a shortage of qualified teachers and clearly needs educators in inland regions. However, the Ministry of Education (MOE) continues to restrict participation by foreign educators and trainers. China permits only non-profit educational activities that do not compete with the MOE-supervised nine years of compulsory education, thereby inhibiting much-needed foreign investment in the education sector. In April 2000, MOE also banned foreign companies and organizations from offering educational services via satellite networks.

In June 2004, the Ministry of Education issued the Implementing Rules for China-Foreign Cooperative Education Projects. Although formulated to implement the Regulations on China-Foreign Cooperation in Running Schools, issued in September 2003, the rules allow foreign educators to participate only in certain activities, including education offering academic certificates, supplementary education and preschool education. These activities cannot take the form of activities at actual educational institutions.

Foreign universities may set up non-profit operations. However, they must have a Chinese university host and partner to ensure that programs bar subversive content and localize imported information.

Meanwhile, China's training market is unregulated, which discourages potential investors from entering the market.

Legal Services

Prior to its WTO accession, China maintained various restrictions in the area of legal services. It prohibited representative offices of foreign law firms from practicing Chinese law or engaging in profit-making activities with regard to non-Chinese law. It also imposed restrictions on foreign law firms' formal affiliation with Chinese law firms, limited foreign law firms to one representative office and maintained geographic restrictions. Chinese law firms, on the other hand, have been able to open offices freely throughout China since 1996.

As part of its WTO accession, China agreed to lift quantitative and geographical restrictions on the establishment of representative offices by foreign law firms within one year after accession. In addition, foreign representative offices are to be able to engage in profit-making business, to advise clients on foreign legal matters and to provide information on the impact of the Chinese legal environment, among other things. They also are to be able to maintain long-term "entrustment" relationships with Chinese law firms and to instruct lawyers in the Chinese law firm as agreed between the two law firms.

The State Council issued the Regulations on the Administration of Foreign Law Firm Representative Offices in December 2001, and the Ministry of Justice issued implementing rules in July 2002. While these measures removed some market access barriers, they also generated concern among foreign law firms doing business in China. In many areas, these measures were ambiguous. For example, it appeared that these measures created an economic needs test for foreign law firms that want to establish offices in China, which would raise concerns regarding China's compliance with its GATS commitments. The measures also seemed to take an overly restrictive view of the types of legal services that foreign law firms may provide. In addition, the procedures for establishing a new office or an additional office were unnecessarily time-consuming. For example, a foreign law firm may not establish an additional representative office until its most recently established representative office has been in practice for three consecutive years. Foreign attorneys also may not take China's bar examination, and they may not hire registered members of the Chinese bar as attorneys.

Although a number of U.S. and other foreign law firms have been able to open a second office in China, little progress has been made on the other problematic aspects of these measures, particularly the economic needs test, the unreasonable restrictions on the types of legal services that can be provided and the unnecessary delays that must be endured when seeking to establish new offices. These obstacles continue to prevent foreign law firms from participating fully in China's legal market.

Accounting and Management Consultancy Services

Prior to China's accession to the WTO, foreign accounting firms could not choose their own Chinese joint venture partners freely or enter into contractual agreements that could fully integrate these joint ventures. Upon its accession to the WTO, China agreed to allow foreign accounting firms to partner with any Chinese entity of their choice. China also agreed to abandon the prohibition on foreign accounting firms' representative offices engaging in profit-making activities. In addition, China agreed that foreign accounting firms could engage in taxation and management consulting services, without having to satisfy the more restrictive requirements on form of establishment applicable to new entities seeking to provide those services separately.

The Chinese Institute of Certified Public Accountants, a government body under MOF, has made progress in modernizing accounting in China. Since China's WTO accession, MOF has released four newly revised auditing statements covering inter-bank confirmation, capital verification, accounting estimates and the audit of commercial bank financial statements. Furthermore, MOF has been active in standardizing accounting procedures across a wide range of topics including investments, inventories, cash flow statements and fixed assets. CSRC, meanwhile, requires a listed company to appoint a certified international CPA firm to conduct audits on prospectuses and annual reports in accordance with international standards.

Despite these positive changes, pervasive problems remain. Differing accounting regulations limit the comparability of data, and the accounting practices followed by many domestic firms do not meet international conventions.

Advertising Services

Prior to China's accession to the WTO, foreign advertising firms had been restricted to representative offices or minority ownership of joint ventures. In its WTO accession agreement, however, China agreed to allow majority foreign ownership of joint venture advertising companies by December 11, 2003, and wholly foreign-owned subsidiaries by December 11, 2005.

In March 2004, SAIC and MOFCOM issued rules governing joint venture, cooperative and wholly foreign-owned advertising firms. To establish branches, a firm must have paid in full its registered capital and have at least RMB20 million ($2.5 million) in annual advertising revenue. Foreign firms are currently limited to a 70 percent share of joint venture and cooperative firms. Implementing rules, effective January 1, 2005, subsequently allowed wholly foreign-owned advertising firms to conduct business in China.

Advertising in China is still governed by China's 1995 Advertising Law, which is enforced by SAIC. Among other things, the law bans messages "hindering the public or violating social customs." The law is also subject to interpretation by SAIC, which must approve all advertising campaigns. One additional difficulty for foreign advertising firms, as well as foreign manufacturers, is that China has strict regulations prohibiting comparative advertising as well as any advertising with claims about the relative superiority of one brand over another. Marketing strategies that are successful in some other countries are therefore illegal in China.

Movement of Professionals

Generally, there are no special entry restrictions placed on U.S. professionals who wish to work in China, such as doctors or engineers. However, like other foreign professionals, they must receive approval from the Foreign Experts Bureau. Prior to arrival, a prospective American job applicant may be asked to provide notarized copies of his or her professional credentials and a summary of past work experience. The credentials will be used by the employer to file for a "foreign experts residency permit" for the American employee. Once the "foreign expert" permit is authorized, the prospective employee can request a work visa (a "Z" visa) from a Chinese embassy or consulate. If the prospective employee arrives in China on a visitors' visa (an "L" visa) prior to commencing employment, the prospective employee is usually asked to depart China prior to starting work, and to apply for the appropriate work visa from a foreign entry point (usually Hong Kong). Local employers are responsible for all employment or income tax and other withholdings for these "foreign experts" while they are employed in China. The government has liberalized access somewhat by issuing "permanent resident" visas to longtime foreign residents of China, which replace the additional "resident cards" previously required.

Chapter 8

INVESTMENT BARRIERS

The volume of foreign investment in China remained high in 2006 despite the introduction of significant new investment barriers. According to the United Nations Conference on Trade and Development, China received $72.4 billion in FDI in 2006, 3 percent less than in 2005. China was the world's third-largest investment destination, after the United States and the United Kingdom. Foreign investors also continued to earn high rates of return in 2006, indicating that China remains an attractive market in which to invest despite the continuing challenges of doing business there. The World Bank Doing Business Report gave China a global ranking for "ease of doing business" of 93 in 2006. Although this ranking was an improvement over China's 108 ranking in 2005, faster progress toward removing investment barriers and reducing government intervention in companies' investment decisions could open new markets to U.S. and other foreign firms, especially in the services sector. In 2006, investors continued to face a lack of transparency, inconsistently enforced laws and regulations, weak IPR protection, corruption and an unreliable legal system incapable of enforcing contracts and judgments.

While China's leadership has repeatedly affirmed its commitment to further open China to foreign investment, China adopted a series of more restrictive foreign investment policies in 2006. These policies indicated that China would be more selective in encouraging foreign investment, more actively targeting higher value-added sectors (including high technology research and development, advanced manufacturing, energy efficiency and modern agriculture and services) rather than basic manufacturing. It also appeared that China would be seeking to spread the benefits of foreign investment beyond China's comparatively wealthy coastal area by encouraging multinationals to establish regional headquarters and operations in Central, Western and Northeast China.

While the United States supports the liberalization of China's investment regime, the United States is concerned about the recent increase in proposed and adopted measures that restrict investment. Often, these restrictions are accompanied by other problematic industrial policies, such as the increased use of subsidies, preferences for using domestic rather than imported goods and the development of China-specific standards. Many of these developments appear to represent protectionist tools by industrial planners to shield inefficient or monopolistic enterprises from competition, counter to the market-oriented principles that have been the basis for much of China's economic success.

Investment Requirements

Upon its accession to the WTO, China assumed the obligations of the Agreement on Trade-Related Investment Measures (TRIMS Agreement), which prohibits investment measures that violate GATT Article III obligations to treat imports no less favorably than domestic products or the GATT Article XI obligation not to impose quantitative restrictions on imports. The TRIMS Agreement thus expressly requires elimination of measures such as those that require or provide benefits for the incorporation of local inputs (known as local content requirements) in the manufacturing process, or measures that restrict a firm's imports to an amount related to its exports or related to the amount of foreign exchange a firm earns (known as trade balancing requirements). In its WTO accession agreement, China also specifically agreed to eliminate export performance, local content and foreign exchange balancing requirements from its laws, regulations and other measures, and not to enforce the terms of any contracts imposing these requirements. In addition, China agreed that it would no longer condition importation or investment approvals on these requirements or on requirements such as technology transfer and offsets.

Although China has revised many laws and regulations to conform to its WTO investment commitments, some of the revised laws and regulations continue to "encourage" technology transfer, without formally requiring it. U.S. companies remain concerned that this "encouragement" in practice can amount to a "requirement" in many cases, particularly in light of the high degree of discretion provided to Chinese government officials when reviewing investment applications. Similarly, some laws and regulations "encourage" exportation or the use of local content. Moreover, according to U.S. companies, some Chinese government officials in 2006 – even in the absence of encouraging language in a law or regulation – still consider factors such as export performance and local content when deciding whether to approve an investment or to recommend approval of a loan from a Chinese policy bank, which is often essential to the success of an investment project.

Investment Guidelines

Foreign Investment Catalogue

China's foreign investment objectives are primarily defined through its Foreign Investment Catalogue, which is revised every few years and supplemented by directives from various government agencies. Revisions to the catalogue and contradictions between it and other pronouncements have confused investors and added to the perception that the investment guidelines do not provide a stable basis for business planning. The resulting uncertainty as to which industries are being promoted as investment targets and for how long undermines confidence in the stability of the investment climate.

China's most recent revisions to the catalogue took effect January 1, 2005. Investment in unlisted sectors is considered "permitted," while China "encourages" investment in sectors where it believes it benefits from foreign assistance or technology transfers. Furthermore, investment is "restricted" in sectors that do not meet "the needs of China's national economic development." In these instances, foreign firms must form joint ventures with Chinese firms and restrict their equity ownership to a minority share if they want to invest in China.

China "prohibits" foreign investment in sectors that it views as key to its national security, such as news agencies, radio and television broadcasting stations and networks, radio and television programming, film production and screening, and the publication, importation and wholesale distribution of press and audiovisual products. The production of arms and the mining and processing of certain minerals by foreign investors are also prohibited. In addition, U.S. investors have expressed concern about China's prohibition of investment in the production and development of biotechnology plant seeds.

Since 2004, provincial governments have enjoyed expanded authority to directly approve many foreign investment projects. Currently, in "encouraged" and "permitted" sectors, proposed foreign investments valued above $500 million require NDRC review and State Council approval. Furthermore, foreign projects in "restricted" sectors valued above $50 million require similar central government review and approval.

China uses a variety of incentives to encourage foreign investment in targeted sectors, like high technology industries, such as duty-free import of capital equipment and VAT rebates on inputs. Foreign investors in targeted regions and special economic zones and in certain industries, such as machinery and construction, also benefit from reduced income taxes, although in December 2006 the National People's Congress began considering a draft enterprise income tax law that could eliminate many of these tax advantages.

Administrative Measures to Restrict Investment

In 2006, Chinese regulators announced several measures that limit the ability of foreign firms to participate in investment in China's market.

For example, in June 2006, the State Council issued the Opinions on the Revitalization of the Industrial Machinery Manufacturing Industries, which calls for China to expand the market share of domestic companies involved in 16 types of equipment manufacturing, including large equipment for clean and efficient power generation, critical semiconductor manufacturing equipment, civilian aircraft and aircraft engines, pollution control equipment, textiles machinery and large excavators. This measure advocates a variety of policy supports, such as preferential import duties on parts needed for research and development, encouraging domestic procurement of major technical equipment, a dedicated capital market financing fund for domestic firms and strict review of imports. This measure also suggests that China will implement controls on foreign investments in the industrial machinery manufacturing industries, including a requirement for administrative approval when foreign entities seek majority ownership or control of leading domestic firms.

In August 2006, MOFCOM and five other government agencies issued the Provisions of Acquisition of Domestic Enterprises by Foreign Investment, which became effective September 2006. This measure revised existing rules for mergers and acquisitions involving foreign investors and, among other things, established a legal basis for a "national economic security" review process that can block proposed transactions. Under the new rules, foreign mergers and acquisitions of domestic enterprises that would result in "actual control" of a domestic enterprise in a "key industry" with "potential impact on national economic security" or that would alter control of a famous Chinese trademark or brand require MOFCOM approval. The new rules also place MOFCOM in the role of determining if the domestic acquisition target has been appropriately valued and allow MOFCOM to initiate an anti-monopoly investigation if "large market shares" are involved or if market competition is "materially" affected. Although implementing measures have not yet been issued, foreign investors have already found that they face greater difficulties purchasing controlling stakes in prominent Chinese firms, and several proposed transactions have stalled. In one positive development, the new rules do now permit the use of foreign shares as consideration for the acquisition of Chinese companies, a change that could facilitate foreign investment in China.

Subsequently, in November 2006, the NDRC released a Five-Year Plan on foreign investment, which promised greater scrutiny over foreign capital utilization. The plan calls for the realization of a "fundamental shift" from "quantity" to "quality" in foreign investment during the period from 2006 to 2010. The state's focus would change from shoring up domestic capital and foreign exchange shortfalls to introducing advanced technology, management expertise and talent. In addition, more attention would be paid to ecology, environment and energy efficiency. The plan also demands tighter tax supervision of foreign enterprises, and it seeks to restrict foreign firms' acquisition of "dragon head" enterprises, to prevent the "emergence or expansion of foreign capital monopolies," to protect national economic security and to prevent the "abuse of intellectual property."

In December 2006, the State Assets Supervision and Administration Commission (SASAC) issued the Guiding Opinion Concerning the Advancement of Adjustments of State Capital and the Restructuring of State-Owned Enterprises, which identified an expansive list of sectors deemed critical to the national economy. This measure explained that "pillar" and "backbone" industries such as automotive, chemical, construction, electronic information, equipment manufacturing, iron and steel, non-ferrous metal, science and technology, and survey and design must maintain relatively strong state control. Reportedly, SASAC officials also identified a separate set of seven strategic sectors in which state capital must play a leading role, including aviation, coal, defense, electric power and grid, oil and petrochemicals, shipping, and telecommunications. It remains unclear how SASAC will implement these policies.

In 2006, China also continued to employ various sector-specific measures designed to impose new requirements on foreign investors. Measures affecting foreign investment in the automotive and steel sectors are discussed above in the section on Import Substitution Policies.

Other Investment Issues

Venture Capital

In March 2003, new regulations took effect permitting the establishment of foreign-invested venture capital firms, including wholly foreign-owned enterprises, aimed at funding high technology and new technology startups in industries open to foreign investment. These regulations lowered capital requirements, allowed foreign-invested firms to manage funds directly invested from overseas, and offered the option of establishing venture capital firms in a form similar to the limited liability partnerships used in other countries.

Meanwhile, regulations that took effect in April 2001 permitted foreign private equity firms subject to limits on corporate structure, share issuance and transfers, and investment exit options. These same regulations, however, bar all domestic and foreign securities firms from the private equity business.

Investment exit problems, especially the difficulty of listing on China's stock exchanges, coupled with the bureaucratic approvals required to list overseas, have limited interest in establishing China-based venture capital and private equity investment. As a result, most foreign venture capital and private equity investments in China are actually housed in offshore investment entities, which, as with other offshore FDI, can be transferred without Chinese government approval.

The Chinese government issued new regulations for domestic venture capital firms in the fall of 2005, and implementing rules went into effect on March 1, 2006. It is unclear if foreign firms choosing to operate onshore will be allowed to take advantage of the incentives offered to domestic firms.

Holding Companies

China has relaxed some restrictions on the scope and operations of holding companies, although minimum capital requirements normally make the establishment of a holding company suitable only for corporations with several large investments. Holding companies may manage human resources across their affiliates and also provide certain market research and other services. However, some restrictions on services provided by holding companies and on holding companies' financial operations and the ability to balance foreign exchange internally remain in place. Profit and loss consolidation within holding companies also remains prohibited.

China has begun to open its domestic equity markets to investments from foreign firms. Through the Qualified Foreign Institutional Investor (QFII) program, foreign securities firms may apply for QFII status, which permits limited access to the RMB-denominated A-share market. As of October 2006, China had granted QFII status to 50 foreign entities, 41 of which had obtained quotas totaling $8.2 billion.

Access to Capital Markets

Foreign-invested firms in China are often unable to access domestic and international stock markets, to sell corporate bonds and equity, or to engage in normal merger, acquisition and divestment activity. In addition, foreign exchange transactions on China's capital account can be concluded only with case-bycase official review, and approvals are tightly regulated. However, recent regulations permitting greater capital outflows and pronouncements by Chinese government officials encouraging Chinese firms to invest abroad suggest that China now recognizes that continued large capital inflows are not sustainable. To date, foreign firms remain generally satisfied because they are able to repatriate profits. At the same time, most major foreign firms prefer to reinvest their profits, not exit the Chinese market.

Chapter 9

GOVERNMENT PROCUREMENT

The WTO Agreement on Government Procurement (GPA) is a plurilateral agreement and currently covers the United States and 39 other WTO Members that have joined it. The GPA applies to the procurement of goods and services by central and sub-central government entities listed by each party, subject to thresholds and certain exceptions. It requires GPA parties to provide MFN and national treatment to the goods, services and suppliers of other GPA parties and to apply detailed procedures designed to ensure fairness and predictability in the procurement process.

At present, China is not a party to the GPA. It committed to become an observer to the GPA upon its WTO accession, and in February 2002, it became an observer to the WTO Committee on Government Procurement. China also committed, in its WTO accession agreement, to initiate negotiations for accession to the GPA "as soon as possible." Following sustained U.S. engagement, China agreed at the April 2006 JCCT meeting that it would initiate GPA negotiations by no later than December 2007.

Until it joins the GPA, China has committed in its WTO accession agreement that all of its central and local government entities will conduct their procurements in a transparent manner. China also agreed that, if it opened a procurement to foreign suppliers, it would provide MFN treatment by allowing all foreign suppliers an equal opportunity to participate in the bidding process.

In June 2002, China adopted its Government Procurement Law, which became effective in January 2003. This law attempts to follow the spirit of the GPA and incorporates provisions from the United Nations Model Law on Procurement of Goods. The law also directs central and sub-central government entities to give priority to "local" goods and services, with limited exceptions, as

China is permitted to do, because it is not yet a party to the GPA. China envisions that this law will improve transparency, reduce corruption and lower government costs. This law is also seen as a necessary step toward reforming China's government procurement system in preparation for China eventually becoming a party to the GPA. It is notable, however, that the Government Procurement Law does not cover tendering and bidding for public works projects, which represent at least one-half of China's government procurement market. Those projects are subject to a different regulatory regime, which will have to be brought into compliance with the GPA before China accedes to the GPA.

China began the process of drafting regulations implementing the Government Procurement Law soon after its issuance in June 2002. MOF issued these regulations – the Measures on the Administration of Bidding for Government-Procured Goods and Services – in August 2004. They set out detailed procedures for the solicitation, submission and evaluation of bids for government contracts relating to goods and services and help to clarify the scope and coverage of the Government Procurement Law. MOF also issued several sets of implementing rules, including measures relating to the announcement of government procurements and the handling of complaints by suppliers relating to government procurement.

Meanwhile, beginning in 2003, U.S. companies expressed concerns about implementing rules on government software procurement being drafted by MOF. At a time when China's already large software market was projected to grow by more than 50 percent annually, the initial draft of these rules reportedly contained guidelines mandating that central and local governments – the largest purchasers of software in China – purchase only software developed in China to the extent possible. In response, the United States organized an industry roundtable to inform the relevant Chinese ministries of the views and concerns of interested U.S. trade associations. U.S. industry officials explained that the creation of a domestic software industry cut off from global standards would lead to inefficiencies and would limit, rather than promote, the development of China's software industry. Working closely with U.S. industry, the United States also submitted written comments on the software procurement proposal and followed up by strongly reiterating its concerns with China during a series of bilateral meetings. The United States was concerned not only about U.S. software exporters continuing access to China's large and growing market for packaged and custom software – \$7.5 billion in 2004 – but also about the precedent that could be established for other sectors if China proceeded with MOF's proposed restrictions on the purchase of foreign software by central and local governments. At the July 2005 JCCT meeting, China took note of the United States' strong concerns and indicated that it would indefinitely suspend the drafting of implementing rules on government software procurement.

Soon afterwards, however, the issue of preferences for the purchase of domestic goods again appeared, when the State Council issued China's Medium to Long Term Science and Technology Master Plan in early 2006. The NDRC and several other ministries and agencies are in charge of developing regulations to implement this strategy, which includes preferences for the purchase of domestic goods as an important industrial policy tool. The United States is concerned that these regulations may unfairly discriminate against U.S. firms and is therefore closely monitoring developments in this area.

A similar issue arose in December 2005, when China issued a measure announcing that products incorporating the WAPI standards should be given preference in government procurement. This measure is discussed above in the "Standards, Technical Regulations and Conformity Assessment Procedures" section.

Chapter 10

ELECTRONIC COMMERCE

China has experienced dramatic growth in Internet usage since 1999. According to the 19th Internet survey recently published by the China Internet Network Information Center (CNNIC), the number of Internet users in China reached approximately 137 million at the end of 2006, representing an increase of 23 percent over the previous year, second only to the United States in terms of total users. Falling personal computer prices and the arrival of devices tailored for the Chinese market will further expand Internet access.

China has also experienced a dramatic increase in the number of domain names established. By the end of 2006, there were more than 4.1 million registered domain names in China. Of this total, there were more than 1.8 million domain names registered under ".cn", representing a 64 percent increase over the previous year. However, despite these developments, CNNIC reported that only 24 percent of surveyed Chinese Internet users frequently use the Internet for online shopping services. Nevertheless, China is experiencing the rapid development of online businesses such as search engines, network education, online advertisements, audio-video service, paid e-mail, short message, online job hunting, Internet consulting, e-trading and online gaming.

The Chinese government recognizes the potential of electronic commerce to promote exports and increase competitiveness and has made some progress toward establishing a viable commercial environment. However, some Chinese ministries with responsibility for electronic commerce have excessively regulated the Internet, thereby stifling the free flow of information and the consumer privacy needed for electronic commerce to flourish. Content is still controlled and encryption regulated, as discussed more fully above (in the "Online Services" section).

A number of technical problems also inhibit the growth of electronic commerce in China. Rates charged by government-approved Internet service providers make Internet access expensive for most Chinese citizens. Slow connection speeds are another problem, although this is changing quickly as broadband connections become more readily available. By the end of 2006, nearly 76 percent of China's Internet users had broadband connections, representing an increase of 18 percentage points over 2005, and China Telecom is now reportedly the world's largest digital subscriber line, or DSL, operator. There are now 104 million broadband subscribers in China. China surpassed Japan in 2004 as the country with the second most broadband lines after the United States. At the same time, Internet penetration remains relatively low in China, and there is a large urban/rural divide in penetration rates (the urban penetration rate is six times higher than the rural penetration rate as of July 2006), so there is still significant room for growth.

Other impediments to Chinese businesses and consumers conducting online transactions include the paucity of credit payment systems, consumer reluctance to trust online merchants, the lack of secure online payment systems and inefficient delivery systems. China has also yet to develop a legal framework conducive to the rapid growth of electronic commerce. Laws recognizing the validity of "econtracting" tools and stressing the importance of online privacy and security have been proposed, but not yet issued. Despite these obstacles, however, a large and growing percentage of Chinese Internet users reportedly have made online purchases.

In August 2004, China passed its first electronic commerce legislation, which addressed, among other things, e-signatures. China is reportedly drafting data privacy legislation and regulations that will address online transactions and payments.

Chapter 11

ANTICOMPETITIVE PRACTICES

Competition Policy Laws and Regulations

China maintains many laws and regulations in the competition policy area. China's principal law is the Anti-Unfair Competition Law, enacted by the National People's Congress (NPC) in 1993. This law addresses a variety of matters, as it (a) prohibits firms from using a trademark, name or packaging without a license, as well as false advertising and other practices intended to confuse consumers; (b) outlaws bribery, the purchase or sale of business secrets, and predatory pricing; (c) restricts a firm's ability to tie the sale of one product to another or impose "unreasonable conditions" on purchases; (d) bans collusion and outlaws "spreading false facts" that damage a competitor; and (e) in theory, limits the business practices of legally-authorized monopolies and restricts the government's ability to require that private firms engage in certain commercial transactions with state-owned enterprises.

China maintains some laws and regulations that limit competition. For example, the national government has legislated that production in certain sectors be concentrated in monopolies, near monopolies or authorized oligopolies. As in some other countries, these enterprises are concentrated in capital intensive sectors, like electricity and transportation, or in industries such as fixed-line telephony and postal services, in which this approach may be used to ensure national coverage. Some of the key laws and regulations include the Law on Electricity (1996), Civil Aviation Law (1995), Regulations on Telecommunication (2000), Postal Law (1986), Railroad Law (1991) and Commercial Bank Law (amended in 2003), among others. The enforcement of these laws and regulations is uneven as a result of the challenges inherent in attempting to coordinate their implementation nationally and as a result of inconsistent local and provincial enforcement. As China further reforms its economy, it is expected that many of these laws will be revised.

More troubling are efforts by government authorities at all levels in China to regulate competition with specific firms, often state-owned enterprises. Official statements often suggest that these efforts are tied primarily to employment concerns. However, the ultimate beneficiaries of the resulting protectionist measures are often unclear. In addition, local governments frequently enact rules that restrict interprovincial trade. Because the central government has difficulty enforcing its own competition policy measures at the local level, these local government rules continue to restrict market access for certain imported products, raise production costs and limit market opportunities for foreign-invested enterprises.

In June 2006, the NPC conducted the first of the three required readings of a draft Anti-Monopoly Law, which has been in development for nearly 15 years. The United States is carefully following the progress of the draft law, which, among other things, would strengthen the central government's ability to tackle locally authorized monopolies. In bilateral meetings, the United States has raised concerns with particular aspects of the draft law, including legal standards for determining whether a firm has a dominant market position and whether it is abusing that position, notification obligations for foreign mergers and acquisitions, the coverage of state enterprises and disciplines on administrative monopolies. The United States has also raised concerns about the proper relationship between intellectual property rights and antimonopoly enforcement, urging that the mere ownership of an intellectual property right not be considered proof of a dominant market position and that a patent owner's simple refusal to license its technology not be viewed as an antimonopoly violation. A second NPC reading has not yet been scheduled.

Measures Restricting Inward Investment

In 2006, China began to revise its policies toward inward investment. While insisting that it remains open to foreign investment, China adopted policies that restrict inward investment in a range of "strategic" sectors, which appear designed to shield domestic enterprises from foreign competition.

As discussed above in the Investment Barriers section, these policies include the State Council's June 2006 Opinions on the Revitalization of the Industrial Machinery Manufacturing Industries, which calls for China to expand the market share of domestic companies in 16 equipment manufacturing industries. In August

2006, the Ministry of Commerce and five other agencies issued revised rules for foreign mergers and acquisitions, which, among other things, establish a vague "national economic security" basis for rejecting proposed deals as well as an anti-monopoly review that can block deals. In November 2006, the NDRC issued a Five-Year Plan on foreign investment that seeks to restrict foreign acquisitions of leading Chinese enterprises, prevent the emergence of foreign capital monopolies, protect industrial security and prevent abuse of intellectual property. Finally, in December 2006, SASAC published an expansive list of "critical economic sectors" in which China should restrict foreign participation.

Some of these measures maintain or create conflicts of interest by assigning regulatory power to agencies that administer state-owned enterprises competing in the same sectors. In addition, key terms in the new policies, such as "national economic security," remain undefined. The opaque standards and ill-defined processes in these measures have introduced additional ambiguity into China's competition policy.

Chapter 12

Other Barriers

Transparency

In its WTO accession agreement, China committed to publish all laws, regulations and other measures that relate to trade matters, including those that affect imports, and generally to provide a reasonable period for commenting on them before implementation. China also agreed to establish or designate an official journal for the publication of these trade-related measures. In addition, China agreed to provide a copy of new trade-related laws, regulations and other measures to the WTO Secretariat in Geneva, translated into one or more of the WTO's official languages (English, French and Spanish) no later than 90 days after implementation. China further agreed to create various enquiry points for its WTO trading partners and foreign businesses to obtain information about these measures.

Various government-owned specialty newspapers routinely carry the texts of government regulations, implementing rules, circulars and announcements. Many government ministries also publish digests or gazettes containing the texts of these measures, both in written form and on their websites. In addition, there has been a proliferation of online news and information services that routinely offer up-to-date news about, and texts of, new laws and regulations. Some services even provide legal-quality English translations by subscription. However, many measures that do not rise to the level of ministry-issued regulations or implementing rules continue to remain unavailable to the public. China's ministries routinely implement policies based on internal "guidance" or "opinions" that are not available to foreign firms. In addition, experimental or informal policies and draft regulations are regarded as internal matters and public access is tightly controlled.

While positive in some respects, the sheer number of outlets through which trade-related measures are published complicates the ability of interested parties to track their development and issuance. In late 2002, China designated the China Foreign Economic and Trade Gazette as the official journal for this purpose. Published by MOFCOM, it came out on a trial basis in October 2002 and as an official publication in January 2003. However, this journal does not carry draft measures for public comment, nor does it consistently carry trade-related measures developed by ministries and agencies other than MOFCOM. The establishment or designation of a single comprehensive journal would enhance the ability of WTO Members to track the drafting, issuance and implementation of trade-related measures. Furthermore, the use of a single journal to request comments on proposed trade-related measures, as envisioned in China's WTO accession agreement, would facilitate the timely notification of comment periods and submission of comments. In March 2006, the State Council issued a notice directing all central, provincial and local government entities to begin sending copies of all of their trade-related measures to MOFCOM for immediate publication in the MOFCOM Gazette. The United States has been monitoring the effectiveness of this notice, both to assess whether all government entities regularly publish their trade-related measures in the MOFCOM Gazette and whether all types of measures are being published. So far, adherence to the State Council's notice is far from complete.

In December 2001, the State Council issued regulations explicitly allowing comment periods and hearings. However, many of China's ministries and agencies continued to follow the practice prior to China's accession to the WTO. The ministry or agency responsible for drafting a new or revised law or regulation will normally consult with and submit drafts to other ministries and agencies, Chinese experts and affected Chinese companies. At times, the responsible ministry or agency will also consult with select foreign companies, although it will not necessarily share drafts with them. As a result, only a small proportion of new or revised laws and regulations have been issued after a period for public comment, and even in these cases the amount of time provided for public comment has generally been short.

In 2004, some improvements took place, particularly on the part of MOFCOM, which began following the rules set forth in its Provisional Regulations on Administrative Transparency, issued in November 2003. Those rules could potentially serve as a model for other ministries and agencies seeking to improve their transparency. Nevertheless, basic compliance with China's notice-and-comment commitment has continued to be uneven. In the area of intellectual property rights, for example, several ministries and agencies circulated proposed measures for public comment in 2005 and 2006. The National People's Congress also circulated a proposed Labor Contract Law for public comment in March 2006. However, China did not provide for public comment on major trade-related laws and regulations, such as the April 2005 Measures on the Importation of Parts for Entire Automobiles, which has since given rise to a WTO dispute brought by the United States, the EC and Canada, CIRC's December 2005 Regulations on the Administration of the Reinsurance Business, August 2006 merger and acquisition regulations, or Xinhua's September 2006 Administrative Measures on News and Information Release by Foreign News Agencies within China. In addition, China did not seek public input on new rules on telecommunications value-added services issued by MII in July 2006, or new rules on qualification requirements for senior managers of insurance companies issued by CIRC in July 2006. The United States and other WTO Members have also been seeking the opportunity to comment on a number of significant new measures, such as the draft Postal Law and the draft Telecommunications Law, so far without success.

Meanwhile, China's ministries and agencies continue to have a much better record when it comes to making new or revised laws and regulations available to the public. In accordance with State Council regulations issued in December 2001, which require the publication of new or amended regulations 30 days before their implementation, almost all new or revised laws and regulations have been available (in Chinese) soon after issuance and prior to their effective date, an improvement over pre-WTO accession practice. Indeed, these laws and regulations are often published not only in official journals, but also on the Internet. At the same time, however, China continues to lag behind in providing translations of these laws and regulations.

U.S. industry continues to report instances where Chinese regulators provide Chinese companies unofficial guidance, which is usually unavailable to foreign entities. In some cases, Chinese officials have provided unpublished documents to interested parties, but this dissemination has been *ad hoc* and based more on personal connections than formal procedures.

In late 2001, MOFCOM's predecessor, MOFTEC, established an enquiry point to provide information on new trade and investment laws, regulations and other measures. Other ministries and agencies have also established formal or informal, subject-specific enquiry points. Since the creation of these various enquiry points, U.S. companies have generally found them to be responsive and helpful, and have generally received timely replies.

Legal Framework

Laws and Regulations

Laws and regulations in China tend to be more general and ambiguous than in other countries. While this approach allows the Chinese authorities to apply laws and regulations flexibly, it also results in inconsistency and confusion in application. Companies often have difficulty determining whether their activities contravene a particular law or regulation.

In China, regulations are also promulgated by a host of different ministries and governments at the central, provincial and local levels, and it is not unusual for the resulting regulations to be at odds with each other. Even though finalized regulations are now routinely published in China, they often leave room for discretionary application and inconsistencies, either through honest misunderstanding or by design. Indeed, government bureaucracies have sometimes been accused of selectively applying regulations. China has many strict rules that are often ignored in practice until a person or entity falls out of official favor. Governmental authorities can wield their discretionary power to crack down on foreign or disfavored investors or make special demands on them simply by threatening to crack down.

This lack of a clear and consistent framework of laws and regulations can be a barrier to the participation of foreign firms in the Chinese domestic market. A comprehensive legal framework, coupled with adequate prior notice of proposed changes to laws and regulations and an opportunity to comment on those changes, would greatly enhance business conditions, promote commerce and reduce opportunities for corruption. The U.S. Government has provided technical assistance, at the central, provincial and local levels of government in China, in an effort to promote improvements in China's legislative and regulatory drafting process. In its WTO accession agreement, China committed to establish tribunals for the review of all administrative actions relating to the implementation of trade-related laws, regulations, judicial decisions and administrative rulings. These tribunals must be impartial and independent of the government authorities entrusted with the administrative enforcement in question, and their review procedures must include the right of appeal. To date, little information is publicly available regarding the frequency or outcomes of review before these tribunals.

China also committed, at all levels of government, to apply, implement and administer all of its laws, regulations and other measures relating to trade in goods and services in a uniform and impartial manner throughout China, including in special economic areas. In connection with this commitment, in 2002, China also established an internal review mechanism, now overseen by MOFCOM's

Department of WTO Affairs, to handle cases of non-uniform application of laws. The actual workings of this mechanism remain unclear, however.

Commercial Dispute Resolution

Both foreign and domestic companies often avoid seeking resolution of commercial disputes through the Chinese courts, as skepticism about the independence and professionalism of China's court system and the enforceability of court judgments and awards remains high. There is a widespread perception that judges, particularly outside of China's big cities, are subject to influence by local political or business pressures. Most judges are not trained in the law and/or lack higher education, although this problem decreases at the higher levels of the judiciary.

At the same time, the Chinese government is moving to establish consistent and reliable mechanisms for dispute resolution through the adoption of improved codes of ethics for judges and lawyers and increased emphasis on the consistent and predictable application of laws. The Judges' Law, issued by the Standing Committee of the National People's Congress in 1995, requires judges to have degrees in law or in other subjects where they have acquired specialized legal knowledge, and permits judges appointed before the law's implementation who do not meet these standards to undergo necessary training. In 1999, the Supreme People's Court began requiring judges to be appointed based on merit and educational background and experience, rather than through politics or favoritism. In 2002, the Supreme People's Court issued rules designating certain higher-level courts to hear cases involving administrative agency decisions relating to international trade in goods or services or intellectual property rights. According to the Supreme People's Court, China's more experienced judges sit on the designated courts, and the geographic area under the jurisdiction of each of these designated courts has been broadened in an attempt to minimize local protectionism. The rules provide that foreign or Chinese enterprises and individuals may bring cases in the designated courts raising challenges under the Administrative Litigation Law to decisions made by China's administrative agencies relating to international trade matters. The rules also state that when there is more than one reasonable interpretation of a law or regulation, the courts should choose an interpretation that is consistent with the provisions of international agreements to which China has committed, such as the WTO rules.

Despite initial enthusiasm, foreign observers have grown increasingly skeptical of the China International Economic and Trade Arbitration Commission (CIETAC) as a forum for the arbitration of trade disputes. Some foreign firms have obtained satisfactory rulings from CIETAC but other firms and legal professionals have raised concerns about restrictions on the selection of arbitrators and inadequacies in procedural rules necessary to ensure thorough, orderly and fair management of cases.

Finally, in cases where the judiciary or arbitration panels have issued judgments in favor of foreign-invested enterprises, enforcement of the judgments has often been difficult. Officials responsible for enforcement are often beholden to local interests and unwilling to enforce court judgments against locally powerful companies or individuals.

Labor Issues

In recent years, China has expanded the scope of its national labor laws and regulations so they now cover most, though not all, key labor areas. Even with these changes, China does not adhere to certain internationally recognized labor standards, such as the rights of freedom of association and collective bargaining. There are many reports indicating that China does not enforce its laws and regulations concerning minimum wages, hours of work and occupational safety and health. There are also persistent concerns about the use of prison labor and child labor. In addition, labor laws and regulations are applied inconsistently between Chinese-owned enterprises and foreign-invested enterprises.

The Chinese government is slowly developing nationwide pension, unemployment insurance, medical insurance and workplace injury insurance systems that require substantial employer contributions. These systems are still rudimentary and characterized by serious funding shortfalls, in part due to widespread non-compliance among domestic firms. A Chinese government audit report published in November 2006 reveals that more than RMB7 billion ($875 million) of China's RMB2 trillion ($250 billion) social security funds had been misappropriated. This revelation has made social security the primary concern for many Chinese citizens, according to a subsequent survey.

The cost of labor, especially unskilled labor, is low in much of China. The existence of a large pool of surplus rural workers, many of whom seek work in urban areas, helps to keep unskilled wages low. Some companies offering substandard wages and working conditions have experienced shortages of unskilled labor. Where competition for workers is intense and the supply limited, as in the case of technical, managerial and professional staff in China's coastal areas, wages can be higher. However, restrictions on labor mobility distort labor costs. China is gradually easing restrictions under the country's household registration system, which has traditionally limited the movement of workers within the country, in part due to the recognition that labor mobility is essential to the continued growth of the economy. Reportedly, wages for many migrant workers, especially construction workers, are not paid on a monthly basis as required by China's national labor laws and regulations, but rather at year end. These workers also remain vulnerable to wage arrearages.

In 2005, the China National Textile and Apparel Council established the Committee for the Promotion of Corporate Social Accountability System for Chinese Textile Enterprises (CSC-9000T). Reportedly, increasing numbers of Chinese firms have realized the importance of social accountability but remain confused about the various foreign corporate social accountability standards and certifications bodies that exist. The council formed CSC-9000T to formulate Chinese corporate social responsibility standards to promote among Chinese firms. The standards are based on relevant Chinese legislation and regulations and reference international practices. More than 300 council members have adopted these standards. CSC-9000T is designed as a capacity building program to train members on best practices for complying with Chinese legal standards, rather than an accreditation or audit-based system. Ten members participated in the pilot phase of the CSC-9000T project in 2006, and the organization is now preparing to expand the pilot project to 100 members. The pilot project consists of surveying standards implementation and providing follow-up training for participating companies. CSC-9000T is also working with international Corporate Social Responsibility organizations and buyers to refine the program and publicize its existence.

Corruption

Many people expected that China's entry into the WTO, which mandated a significant reduction in tariffs, would in turn reduce incentives for smuggling-related corruption. While WTO membership has increased China's exposure to international best practices and resulted in some overall improvements in transparency, corruption remains endemic. Chinese officials themselves admit that corruption is one of the most serious problems the country faces, and China's new leadership has called for an acceleration of the country's anti-corruption drive with a focus on closer monitoring of provincial-level officials. According to Chinese state media sources, from January 2003 to August 2006, more than 67,500 government officials were punished for corruption, with approximately 17,000 of those officials being punished for corruption between January 2006 and August 2006. China also launched an anti-corruption campaign in 2006 targeting Communist Party of China officials. According to the Xinhua News Agency, more than 97,000 party officials were punished in 2006.

In July 2004, China implemented a new Administrative Licensing Law. This law is designed to increase transparency in the licensing process, an area that has long served as a source of official corruption. This law seeks to ensure the reasonable use of administrative licensing powers to protect the interests of corporations and individuals and to promote efficient administrative management by requiring government agencies to set up special offices for issuing licenses and to respond to applications within 20 days. Since its 2004 implementation, the law has increased transparency in the licensing process, while reducing procedural obstacles and strengthening the legal environment for domestic and foreign enterprises.

China issued its first law on unfair competition in 1993, and the central government continues to call for improved self-discipline and anti-corruption initiatives at all levels of government. While the central government in recent years has pledged to begin awarding contracts solely on the basis of commercial criteria, it is unclear how quickly and to what extent the government will be able to follow through on this commitment. U.S. suppliers complain that the widespread existence of unfair bidding practices in China puts them at a competitive disadvantage. This dilemma is less severe in sectors where the United States holds clear technological or cost advantages. Corruption nevertheless undermines the long-term competitiveness of both foreign and domestic entities in the Chinese market.

Land Issues

China's constitution specifies that all land is owned in common by all the people. In practice, agricultural collectives, under the firm control of local Communist Party chairmen, distribute agricultural land to the rural poor, while city governments distribute land for residential and industrial use. The State and collectives can either "grant" or "allocate" land use rights to enterprises in return for the payment of fees. Enterprises granted land-use rights are guaranteed compensation if the State asserts eminent domain over the land, while those with allocated rights are not. Granted land-use rights cost more, not surprisingly, than allocated rights. However, the law does not define standards for compensation when eminent domain supersedes granted land-use rights. This situation creates considerable uncertainty when foreign investors are ordered to vacate. The absence of public hearings on planned public projects, moreover, can give affected parties, including foreign investors, little advance warning.

The time limit for land-use rights acquired by foreign investors for both industrial and commercial enterprises is 50 years. A major problem for foreign investors is the array of regulations that govern their ability to acquire land-use rights. Local implementation of these regulations may vary from central government standards, and prohibited practices may occur in one area while they are enforced in another. Most wholly-owned foreign enterprises seek granted land-use rights to state-owned urban land as the most reliable protection for their operations. Chinese-foreign joint ventures usually attempt to acquire granted land-use rights through lease or contribution arrangements with the local partners.

China's current rural land law, which took effect in 2003, gives peasants fixed contracts for periods of 30 years to 50 years and permits peasants to exchange or rent out their land-use rights while their use contract remains in force. There is no immediate prospect for changing from land-use rights to direct ownership of rural land. However, since 2004, China's leadership has pressed for sturdier land rights for farmers along with stricter controls over the legal process for converting farmland from agricultural to industrial or residential use. Local governments are no longer supposed to expropriate land for commercial use, as farmers are now supposed to be able to negotiate a compensation price for land directly with commercial users. However, implementation of these provisions lags.

China's National People's Congress passed a Property Rights Law on March 16, 2007, the first comprehensive legal protection to private property since the founding of the People's Republic in 1949. The property law, which generated years of controversy in the Chinese government but was never published in draft form, reportedly grants equal legal protection to private, state, and collectively owned property. This protection would cover the "means of production," such as factories, but agricultural land would remain a collective possession subject to 30-year leases. It is unclear at this time how the law will be implemented.

INDEX

D

F

G

H

I

T